Math and Nonfiction

Grades 6–8

Math and Nonfiction

Grades 6–8

Jennifer M. Bay-Williams

Sherri L. Martinie

Introduction by

Marilyn Burns

Math Solutions Publications
Sausalito, CA

Math Solutions Publications
150 Gate 5 Road
Sausalito, CA 94965
www.mathsolutions.com

The publisher would like to acknowledge sources of adapted material:

Table of alligator data on page 153 is adapted from *What Happened
to the Mammoths?* by J. Myers (Honesdale, PA: Boyds Mills, 2000), 24.

Instructions for wreath and pinwheel origami on pages 168–70 are adapted from
Connected Mathematics: Kaleidoscopes, Hubcaps, and Mirrors, by G. Lappan, J. T.
Fey, W. M. Fitzgerald, S. N. Friel, and E. D. Phillips (La Porte, IN: Prentice Hall/Dale
Seymour, 1998), 73–75.

List of toy prices on page 182 is adapted from *The All-New Book of Lists for Kids,* by
Sandra Choron and Harry Choron (New York: Houghton Mifflin, 2002), 133–34.

Library of Congress Cataloging-in-Publication Data

Bay-Williams, Jennifer M.
   Math and nonfiction. Grades 6/8 / Jennifer M. Bay-Williams, Sherri L. Martinie ;
   Introduction by Marilyn Burns.
       p. cm.
   Summary: "Provides lessons that link mathematics with nonfiction. Topics include
collecting and analyzing data; using proportional reasoning; and exploring linear and
exponential growth, probability, relationships between two- and three-dimensional
objects, pi, and more. Each lesson includes an overview of the nonfiction title, a
discussion of the lesson's mathematical focus, a description of the activity, and samples
of student work"—Provided by publisher.
   ISBN 978-0-941355-86-5 (alk. paper)
   1. Mathematics—Study and teaching (Middle school) 2. Children's literature in
mathematics education. I. Martinie, Sherri L. II. Title.
   QA135.6.B394 2008
   510.71'2—dc22
                                                              2008024557

Editor: Toby Gordon
Production: Melissa L. Inglis-Elliott
Cover and interior design: Catherine Hawkes/Cat and Mouse
Composition: ICC Macmillan Inc.

Printed in the United States of America on acid-free paper
12 11 10 09 08   SB   1 2 3 4 5

A Message from Marilyn Burns

We at Math Solutions Professional Development believe that teaching math well calls for increasing our understanding of the math we teach, seeking deeper insights into how children learn mathematics, and refining our lessons to best promote students' learning.

Math Solutions Publications shares classroom-tested lessons and teaching expertise from our faculty of Math Solutions Inservice instructors as well as from other respected math educators. Our publications are part of the nationwide effort we've made since 1984 that now includes

- more than five hundred face-to-face inservice programs each year for teachers and administrators in districts across the country;
- annually publishing professional development books, now totaling more than seventy titles and spanning the teaching of all math topics in kindergarten through grade 8;
- four series of videos for teachers, plus a video for parents, that show math lessons taught in actual classrooms;
- on-site visits to schools to help refine teaching strategies and assess student learning; and
- free online support, including grade-level lessons, book reviews, inservice information, and district feedback, all in our *Math Solutions Online Newsletter*.

For information about all of the products and services we have available, please visit our website at *www.mathsolutions.com*. You can also contact us to discuss math professional development needs by calling (800) 868-9092 or by sending an email to *info@mathsolutions.com*.

We're always eager for your feedback and interested in learning about your particular needs. We look forward to hearing from you.

Math Solutions®

Contents

One | Lessons

Two | Additional Ideas

Acknowledgments

We would like to thank the middle school students with whom we have worked; their willingness and eagerness to solve tasks related to the nonfiction we shared were exciting to see.

We wish to thank the teachers who kindly taught lessons, invited us to teach lessons, and contributed ideas and books to be considered for this book. It has been a pleasure!

Teachers from Jefferson County School District, Louisville, Kentucky: Amy Cook, Myers Middle School; Amy English, T. T. Knight Middle School; Lori Brawner, Barret Traditional Middle School; and Cynthia Garwood, J. Graham Brown School.

I would like to also express my sincere appreciation to my entire family, especially Mitch, MacKenna, and Nicolas—thank you for your love and support!

—Jenny

I would like to express my gratitude to my colleagues, friends, and entire family for their continuous support and encouragement. I would especially like to thank my husband, Brian, and our twin boys, Peter and Curtis, who were born while this book was in progress.

—Sherri

Introduction

This book is the latest in our Math Solutions series for teaching mathematics using children's literature, and I'm pleased to present the complete series:

Math and Literature, Grades K–1
Math and Literature, Grades 2–3
Math and Literature, Grades 4–6, Second Edition
Math and Literature, Grades 6–8
Math and Nonfiction, Grades K–2
Math and Nonfiction, Grades 3–5
Math and Nonfiction, Grades 6–8

More than fifteen years ago we published my book *Math and Literature (K–3)*. My premise for that book was that children's books can be effective vehicles for motivating children to think and reason mathematically. I searched for books that I knew would stimulate children's imaginations and that also could be used to teach important math concepts and skills.

After that first book's publication, my colleague Stephanie Sheffield began sending me the titles of children's books she had discovered and descriptions of the lessons she had taught based on them. Three years later, we published Stephanie's *Math and Literature (K–3), Book Two*. And the following year we published Rusty Bresser's *Math and Literature (Grades 4–6)*, a companion to the existing books.

Over the years, some of the children's books we initially included in our resources have, sadly, gone out of print. However, other wonderful titles have emerged. For this new series, we did a thorough review of our three original resources. Stephanie and I collaborated on substantially revising our two K–3 books and reorganizing them into two different books, one for grades K–1 and the other for grades 2–3. Rusty produced a second edition of his book for grades 4–6.

In response to the feedback we received from teachers, we became interested in creating a book that would offer lessons based on children's books for middle school students, and we were fortunate enough to find two wonderful teachers, Jennifer M. Bay-Williams and Sherri L. Martinie, to collaborate on *Math and Literature, Grades 6–8*, bringing the series to four books.

Also in response to teachers, we again increased the series with three additional books that focus on using children's nonfiction books as springboards for lessons. Jamee Petersen created *Math and Nonfiction, Grades K–2*; Stephanie Sheffield built on her experience with the Math and Literature books to team with her colleague Kathleen Gallagher to write *Math and Nonfiction, Grades 3–5*; and Jennifer Bay-Williams and Sherri Martinie created another wonderful resource for middle school teachers, *Math and Nonfiction, Grades 6–8*. We learned that using nonfiction books in math lessons differed from using fiction. Hearing nonfiction books read aloud to them requires children to listen in a different way. Students listen to the facts presented and assimilate that information into what they already know about that particular subject. We learned that rather than read from cover to cover as with fiction, it sometimes makes more sense to read only a portion of a nonfiction book and investigate the subject matter presented in that portion. The authors of our Math and Nonfiction books are sensitive to the demands of nonfiction and how to present new information in order to make it accessible to children.

We're still fond of the lessons that were based on children's books that are now out of print, and we know that through libraries, the Internet, and used bookstores, teachers have access to some of those books. Therefore, we've made all of the older lessons that are not included in the new series of books available online at *www.math solutions.com*. Please visit our website for those lessons and for additional support for teaching math.

I'm pleased and proud to present these books. It was a joy to work on them, and I'm convinced that you and your students will benefit from the lessons we offer.

MARILYN BURNS
2008

Contents Chart

	Lessons	Author of Nonfiction Title	Number	Geometry	Patterns/Algebra	Measurement	Data Analysis/ Probability
1	Scholastic Book of Lists: Fun Facts, Weird Trivia, and Amazing Lists on Nearly Everything You Need to Know!	James Buckley Jr. and Robert Stremme	✔				✔
2	Chocolate: Riches from the Rainforest	Robert Burleigh	✔			✔	✔
3	Cubes, Cones, Cylinders, and Spheres	Tana Hoban		✔			
4	Everybody Loves Ice Cream: The Whole Scoop on America's Favorite Treat	Shannon Jackson Arnold			✔		
5	Fantastic Feats and Failures	Editors of *Yes Mag*		✔	✔		✔
6	Go Figure! A Totally Cool Book About Numbers	Johnny Ball					✔
7	G Is for Googol: A Math Alphabet Book	David M. Schwartz		✔		✔	
8	If You Hopped Like a Frog	David M. Schwartz	✔			✔	
9	The Motley Fool Investment Guide for Teens: Eight Steps to Having More Money Than Your Parents Ever Dreamed Of	David and Tom Gardner	✔		✔		
10	A Negro League Scrapbook	Carole Boston Weatherford	✔				✔
11	One Thousand Paper Cranes: The Story of Sadako and the Children's Peace Statue	Takayuki Ishii		✔	✔		
12	Telling Time	Patricia J. Murphy			✔	✔	✔

	Additional Ideas	Author of Nonfiction Title	Number	Geometry	Patterns/Algebra	Measurement	Data Analysis/Probability
13	200% of Nothing: An Eye-Opening Tour Through the Twists and Turns of Math Abuse and Innumeracy	A. K. Dewdney	✔		✔		✔
14	The All-New Book of Lists for Kids	Sandra and Harry Choron	✔		✔		✔
15	The Breakfast Cereal Gourmet	David Hoffman		✔		✔	
16	Gutsy Girls: Young Women Who Dare	Tina Schwager and Michelle Schuerger			✔		
17	The History of Everyday Life	Elaine Landau	✔				✔
18	If the World Were a Village: A Book About the World's People	David Smith	✔				✔
19	If You Made a Million	David M. Schwartz	✔			✔	
20	The Joy of π	David Blatner		✔		✔	
21	Leonardo's Horse	Jean Fritz		✔	✔	✔	
22	The Librarian Who Measured the Earth	Kathryn Lasky		✔		✔	
23	The Man Who Made Parks: The Story of Parkbuilder Frederick Law Olmsted	Frieda Wishinsky	✔				
24	Made You Look: How Advertising Works and Why You Should Know	Shari Graydon	✔				✔
25	Mathematical Scandals	Theoni Pappas		✔	✔	✔	
26	The Mathematical Universe: An Alphabetical Journey Through the Great Proofs, Problems, and Personalities	William Dunham		✔		✔	
27	Numbers: Facts, Figures and Fiction	Richard Phillips	✔				
28	The Popcorn Book	Tomie de Paola	✔		✔	✔	
29	What Happened to the Mammoths? And Other Explorations of Science in Action	Jack Myers	✔				✔

Part One

Lessons

Scholastic Book of Lists

Fun Facts, Weird Trivia, and Amazing Lists on Nearly Everything You Need to Know!

Scholastic Book of Lists, by James Buckley Jr. and Robert Stremme (2006), contains many facts and trivia, organized by themes. For example, the history section includes lists of presidents, patriotic sayings, and tribes of Native Americans. At the end of each section, there is a survey for students to take that relates back to the facts presented in that section.

The book spans the curricular topics of history, social studies, science, mathematics, languages, and the arts. It also includes lists related to weather, pop culture, sports, and more.

This lesson is about the probability of independent events happening. Students use attribute blocks to explore this concept, then apply what they've learned to figuring out the probability of having both an astrological and a Chinese animal sign in common with one of their peers. Lastly, students find the formula for determining the probability of two independent events.

MATERIALS

attribute blocks, 1 set per small group of students and 1 set for the teacher

grouping circles, made of plastic or string, to create a Venn Diagram

attribute block probabilities record sheets, 1 per small group of students (see Blackline Masters)

overhead transparency of attribute block probabilities record sheet

Introducing the Investigation

I began the lesson by asking students if they knew what their birth sign was. Several students called out their signs. Others were not sure, but using the dates in the *Scholastic Book of Lists*, I helped them figure it out. I asked students what they thought the chance was that someone else in the class had the same birth sign as they did.

I said, "If you think it is likely that someone else has your sign, raise your hand." When students were ready, I called on Wendy and asked her what her sign was.

"Aquarius," she said.

Then I asked who else was an Aquarius. Two other students raised their hands. I did this for two more signs; only one student had the third sign. I explained to the students that we would be looking at the probability that they would have the same astrological signs and Chinese signs as one of their classmates. We figured out that even though there are twelve different Chinese animal signs, each representing certain years, they were all born in only one of three. We discussed that for both of these types of signs, the distribution may not be equal for all possibilities, but that we were going to say they were so we could figure probabilities of equally likely events.

Then I returned to the book and read the topics in the "Grab Bag" section of the book and asked students to select the three they would most like to explore in addition to the first two on astrology and Chinese signs. They picked "gross" food, biggest food, and type of car. I read those lists to students from the "Grab Bag" section of the book (pages 254–73), asking them to write down the foods or cars that made the lists, so that they could pick their choice from among those listed. The entire class was engaged in listening to the lists, groaning at some of the car choices, questioning the gross food options, and expressing awe at how large some of the big foods were. In fact, this introduction lasted more than ten minutes, as students had much to share. (Time could be saved here by selecting only one extra list, as the data for all of these are not needed for the lesson.)

I asked students to look at their choices and to think about how likely it was that someone else in the class had the same answers as they did for each of the five categories. They did not think that this was likely.

I said, "What about having the first two in common—your astrological sign and your Chinese animal sign? That is what we are going to be able to answer at the end of class."

Because students had not explored independent events, I decided to use attribute blocks—a physical model—to illustrate the likelihood of having one trait versus two traits within the set (see Quinn 2001 for more on using attributes to develop a conceptual understanding of probability). First, students had to become familiar with the attribute blocks.

To do this, I set a Venn diagram on the floor using plastic grouping circles (string can also be used). Each circle is about the size of a hula hoop. I labeled one circle *Big* and the other one *Yellow*. I held up two attribute blocks that were different from each other and asked students to tell me four ways we could describe the shapes.

"Color," Lisa said.

"Shape," Cassandra added.

"How about size?" James asked.

I asked, "What are the size choices?"

"Big and small," James replied.

"There is one more thing. Can you see it?" I asked, holding the shapes so that the students could see the thickness.

"Thick or thin," several students replied.

I held up a big circular block and asked where it would go in the Venn diagram. I allowed students time to look at the Venn diagram and then raise their hands. "Whisper to your neighbor where it goes," I instructed. Students agreed it went in the *Big* section of the diagram, but not in the overlap. We continued with five more blocks, deciding where each belonged.

I asked, "If we were to place all of the attribute blocks in our Venn diagram, how many would end up in the *Big* circle? Talk to your partners." After some discussion, students reported back that they thought half would go in that circle because half of the shapes were big and half were small. I asked the same question for yellow, and since the blocks came in three colors, this question was not as easy for the class to answer.

"I think it would be twenty percent because there are less yellow," offered Chris.

"I think ten out of ten because I think they are all yellow," Amy said.

"No, it's one-third because there are three colors, so one in three is yellow," argued Margot.

"Oh, yeah, I was just thinking of the ones in the circle," Amy said. "Of the whole set, there would be only one in three that is yellow, not ten."

I gave instructions to the students for their small-group work. I explained that for each of the possible attributes we had talked about, they were to find the probability of picking a block to match that specific attribute. "For example," I continued, "if you randomly picked a piece, what would the probability be that it was small or that it was red?" I asked one person from each group to get an attribute set and told students to use the blocks to help them find the probabilities.

Before finding these probabilities, I asked students to spend two minutes looking at their blocks and to watch for my hand to go up as a cue that I was ready to ask questions about the blocks. I directed them to see if they could come up with a combination of size, thickness, color, and shape for which no piece existed.

When students got their blocks, they began to sort them by a characteristic. Some groups found all the shapes and then made stacks by color. Other groups created arrays, where the rows were all one shape and the columns were organized by shape, size, and then thickness. Several groups noticed that they were missing a shape or had an extra block. I stopped the groups to clarify that they should each have sixty shapes, none of the blocks should be the same as another block, and they should have five shapes, three colors, two thicknesses, and two sizes. Once they had finished sorting, students figured out that there was exactly one shape for each combination of four traits; for example, there is exactly one big, red, thick square.

I distributed one Attribute Block Probabilities record sheet to each group and placed the transparency of the record sheet on the overhead. We briefly discussed the notation for probability; for example, writing P(red) to mean *What is the probability of red?* I asked each student to record his group's findings in his own notebook as well as recording together on the group record sheet.

Observing the Students

Because of our discussion prior to using the attribute blocks, the students had no trouble identifying that there were twenty red shapes. Many groups figured this out by counting, not by knowing that twenty is one-third of sixty, a strategy that some students did use. Most students did take this shortcut with the attribute *thick*, as they knew that half the blocks were thick and that half of sixty is thirty.

In one group, students were beginning to work on P(red and thick). Nathan added the following two fractions:

$$\frac{20}{60} + \frac{30}{60} = \frac{50}{60}$$

Emily said, "Fifty over sixty; that seems like a lot."

Nathan replied, "Well, I just added the red and the thick; red and thick equals fifty over sixty."

Emily countered, "But there aren't fifty pieces that are red and thick."

During this discussion, Andre was sorting the pieces, finding all the blocks that were red and thick. So far, he had found ten. "There are ten," he stated.

"OK, so ten," Nathan said and recorded that in his notebook.

I interjected, "Why is it not fifty?"

I got puzzled looks, so I restated my question. "If you look at the process Nathan was using, adding thirty and twenty, why doesn't that turn out to be the number of pieces that are thick and red?"

Math and Nonfiction, Grades 6–8

"Because you can't add them together," Nathan offered in a questioning manner.

Emily added, "It's because you aren't just putting together red ones with thick ones because some are the same."

"So, some are the same?" I probed. "Which ones are the same?"

They all studied their pieces. "The ones that are red and thick are the same."

"Oh," said Andre, "adding gets the shapes that are red but includes thin ones, and the thick is also counting all the colors, so you can't just add them."

I could see they were making progress and left them after saying, "Keep thinking about how you can use the first two answers to help you find the third . . . good thinking here."

In another group, Terence, Charles, and Karyn had found all three answers for the first two investigations, each time by just finding the pieces and counting them. They were moving on to the third investigation, in which they would invent their own combinations. I asked them to pause and look at the work they had done, then tell me how they had found the probability of a block sharing two traits.

Terence said, "We just made piles and counted."

I said, "Let's see if you can be clever and avoid some counting. Look back at the second example. How could you just know how many are thin?"

"Well, we did know on that one because thirty is half of sixty and so there were thirty thin."

"And could you use that strategy for square?"

After a pause, Charles said, "Well, there are five shapes."

"So we can divide sixty by five?" Karyn asked.

"Oh, yeah, sixty divided by five is twelve and there were twelve squares," Charles said with confidence.

"What about your simplified fractions? How can you tie those in to your thinking about shortcuts?" I asked.

"Our fraction for squares equals one-fifth . . . oh, there are five shapes, so one in five," said Terence, still pondering if this was a coincidence or not.

"Good thinking here," I said. "Keep looking for those clever ways to figure out the probability, because when we share I will be asking for strategies for finding the probability of two traits."

A Whole-Class Discussion

After about twenty minutes, most groups were completely done, but some had not gotten to the third investigation, which I had actually designed as an extra challenge for the quicker groups. (See Figures 1–1 and 1–2.)

Figure 1–1: This group finished all three investigations.

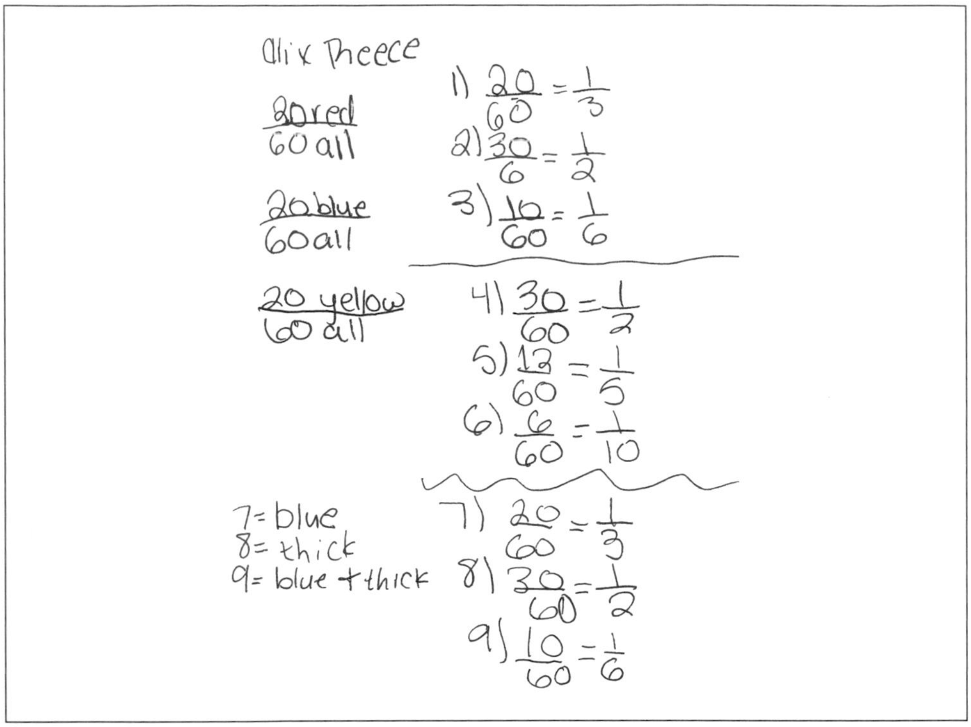
Alix Reece

20 red / 60 all

20 blue / 60 all

20 yellow / 60 all

1) $\frac{20}{60} = \frac{1}{3}$

2) $\frac{30}{6} = \frac{1}{2}$

3) $\frac{10}{60} = \frac{1}{6}$

4) $\frac{30}{60} = \frac{1}{2}$

5) $\frac{12}{60} = \frac{1}{5}$

6) $\frac{6}{60} = \frac{1}{10}$

7= blue
8= thick
9= blue + thick

7) $\frac{20}{60} = \frac{1}{3}$

8) $\frac{30}{60} = \frac{1}{2}$

9) $\frac{10}{60} = \frac{1}{6}$

Figure 1–2: This group expressed the probabilities using both fractions and percents.

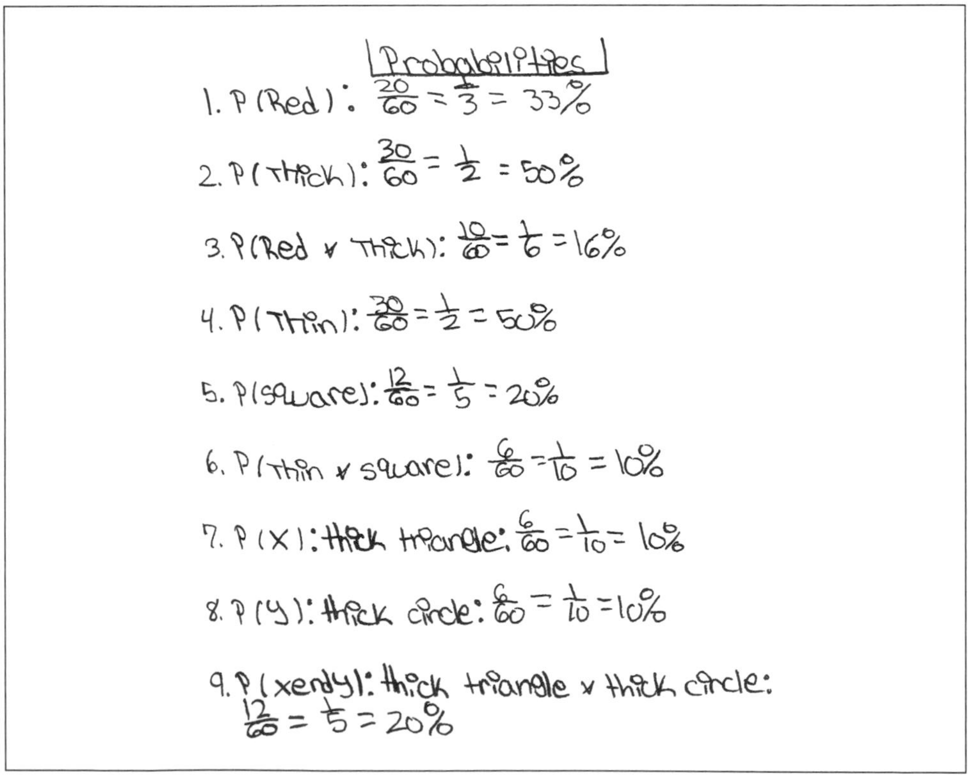
Probabilities

1. P(Red): $\frac{20}{60} = \frac{1}{3} = 33\%$
2. P(thick): $\frac{30}{60} = \frac{1}{2} = 50\%$
3. P(Red + Thick): $\frac{10}{60} = \frac{1}{6} = 16\%$
4. P(Thin): $\frac{30}{60} = \frac{1}{2} = 50\%$
5. P(square): $\frac{12}{60} = \frac{1}{5} = 20\%$
6. P(thin + square): $\frac{6}{60} = \frac{1}{10} = 10\%$
7. P(X): thick triangle: $\frac{6}{60} = \frac{1}{10} = 10\%$
8. P(Y): thick circle: $\frac{6}{60} = \frac{1}{10} = 10\%$
9. P(xandy): thick triangle + thick circle: $\frac{12}{60} = \frac{1}{5} = 20\%$

I asked students to put their attribute blocks away and turn their chairs to face the front of the room. For each of the nine categories on their record sheet, I asked students to tell me what they had recorded as their answers, both the fraction with a denominator of sixty and the simplified fraction. I asked students to talk about patterns they noticed in finding the probability of two attributes. Several students raised their hands.

"If you just multiply the denominators, you get the probability of the two," Deanna stated.

"Can you explain what you mean on the first set?" I asked, seeing that this was not clear to others in the class.

"Well, the probability of red was one-third and the probability of thick was one-half, so multiply the three by the two and you get six. The probability of red and thick was one-sixth. That is our pattern."

"What do the rest of you think about this?" I asked, leading them to the real question I wanted to get to.

"Yes, it works," said Samantha. "I checked the second example, too."

"Why does this work?" I asked. The class was silent for some time.

"Let's see," I said, "if we take the first example, there is a one-in-three chance it is red." I picked up a red block. "What are my chances of picking red?"

"One-third," some students responded.

"OK, so in my set of red, how many of those pieces are thick?" I asked.

"Half," many of the students said.

I could see this discussion wasn't getting where it needed to. I referred the students back to the unsimplified fractions and asked, "How does the fraction for red compare with the fraction for red and thick?"

"Oh, I get it," said Reta. "It's half as much because half of the red are thick. So twenty out of sixty becomes ten out of sixty."

"So for the square, twelve-sixtieths of the shapes are square, but only half of those are thin, so only six-sixtieths are thin and square, right?" Samantha asked.

I could see that students could use the shortcut, but very few were getting the conceptual connection. I asked students to record the patterns that they had found, knowing we would return to this idea again. (See Figures 1–3 through 1–6.)

> 6. If you have 2 things Red & Thick it is less likely that there is going to be a match but there is going to be at least on match.
> :)

Figure 1–3: This student explained an important concept, that there is a lower probability when looking for two attributes.

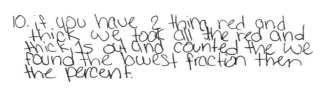

> 10. if you have 2 thing red and thick we took all the red and thick is out and counted the we found the lowest fraction then the percent.

Figure 1–4: This student found all the pieces that fit the attributes and then found the fraction and percent.

Figure 1–5: This student explained a pattern in probabilities that looked like multiplication of fractions.

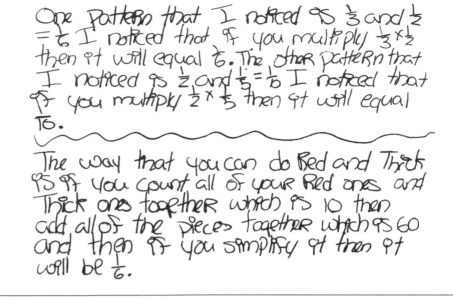

One pattern that I noticed is $\frac{1}{3}$ and $\frac{1}{2}$ = $\frac{1}{6}$ I noticed that if you multiply $\frac{1}{3} \times \frac{1}{2}$ then it will equal $\frac{1}{6}$. The other pattern that I noticed is $\frac{1}{2}$ and $\frac{1}{3}$ = $\frac{1}{6}$ I noticed that if you multiply $\frac{1}{2} \times \frac{1}{3}$ then it will equal $\frac{1}{6}$.

The way that you can do Red and Thick is if you count all of your Red ones and Thick ones together which is 10 then add all of the pieces together which is 60 and then if you simplify it then it will be $\frac{1}{6}$.

Figure 1–6: This student found all red and then found the thick red to figure out the probability.

To find the probability of getting red and thick is to get all the red shape. If you get thick ones and you have all red and thick $^{10}/_{60} = ^1/_6$.

Applying Their Findings

I wanted to see if the students could connect what they had done so far to the prompt at the start of class, so I asked them to go back to their data from the lists in the book. "What is the probability of someone being a Taurus?" I asked.

"One in twelve," they replied.

I asked, "Is it likely we have more than one of those in the class?" Students nodded and said yes. "Raise your hand if you are a Taurus," I directed. Two students raised their hands.

Next I said, "Since you were all born within the same three years, what is the probability of having the same Chinese animal sign?" We were assuming the spread was even, although it wasn't.

"One-third," Melinda said.

I recorded these two probabilities on the board:

$$\text{P}(\textit{astrology sign}) = \frac{1}{12}$$
$$\text{P}(\textit{Chinese animal sign}) = \frac{1}{3}$$

I instructed students to talk to their partners about how likely it would be to have two students in our class with a match for both—for example, if two students were both a Taurus and a Dog. Students discussed this in pairs for several minutes. Several groups made the connection to the strategy they used during the investigations with attribute blocks.

"We think it is one–thirty-sixth because we multiplied the denominators," said Lawrence.

"Yes, we did the same thing—multiplied them," Samuel added.

"Why is this the case? Who can tell me why it makes sense to multiply the denominators?" I asked.

"It's because there are only twelve possibilities for your sign, but then only some of those have the Chinese animal, only one in three," Samantha articulated.

I asked students, "Is it likely that someone else in here has the same two signs that you have?" They had many ideas to offer; most said it was not likely. I asked one student for her signs and asked if anyone else had both of them. No one did. On our fourth try, we did find a match. Everyone wanted to know if he or she had a match, but we had to bring the lesson to a close.

This lesson was excellent in allowing students to make the connections between physical models and the concept of the probability of two events happening at the same time. They learned that with more events, the likelihood goes down. Students were heavily reliant on the models to think through the probability of two events. Some students made the connection from the models to the mathematics of multiplying the probability of each independent event; however, more experiences were needed for most of the class to make this connection.

Chocolate

Riches from the Rainforest

Each two-page spread of *Chocolate: Riches from the Rainforest*, by Robert Burleigh (2002), explains an aspect in the development of chocolate, such as who actually discovered chocolate, how chocolate was first consumed, when sugar was added to it, and when it changed from a liquid to a solid. In addition to highlighting the contributions made by the Mayans, Spaniards, and Americans, the book describes chocolate in today's world, including the production of chocolate chips, the focus of this lesson.

To promote number sense and an understanding of perimeter and area, students are asked to create a visual for illustrating what fifty-eight thousand chocolate chips might look like. Specifically, they explore what that many chocolate chips could surround and what the chips could cover. Students also create a formula to describe chocolate chip production and use the formula to determine how long it would take to produce a million, a billion, and a trillion chocolate chips.

At the end of this lesson are additional ideas that take advantage of the wide range of chocolates that are available. Using the attributes of chocolate candy bars, students determine all possible combinations and explore probability ideas.

MATERIALS

sticky notes, 1 per student

small bags of chocolate chips, such as Kissables, 1 per small group of students

chipping away at chocolate chips record sheets, 1 per student (see Blackline Masters)

rulers or meter sticks marked in both centimeters and inches, 1 per small group of students

calculators, 1 per student

optional: a computer with internet access, for looking up selected data

Introducing the Investigation

I began the lesson by telling the students that they were going to have a quiz, but the good news was it was on something they all knew about—chocolate. I asked students to number their papers from *1 to 6* and then had then make predictions about each of these questions:

Do You Know Chocolate?

- Where does chocolate come from?

- What was the first culture to enjoy chocolate?

- When was it discovered?

- When was a candy bar first made and by whom?

- How many Tootsie Rolls are made in a day?

- How many chocolate chips are made in an hour?

I asked each student to rewrite the answer to the last question on a sticky note, large enough so it could be seen across the room. I had the students hold up their stickies and look at their classmates' estimates. I then began to read *Chocolate: Riches from the Rainforest*. Because of the length of the class period, I skipped some pages, but I was sure to read the pages and passages that addressed the questions I had asked the class. Students were fascinated with many of the facts. As I read, I paused at certain points to ask questions, such as, "Who created the first solid chocolate?" The students guessed Hershey, which is correct. In total I read aloud the following excerpts: the first six pages of the book, which include an introduction, "Where does chocolate come from?" and "Who figured it out?" and pages 15–20 (beginning with "Chocolate conquered Europe . . ." and ending with "Chocolate is here to stay!").

Once I finished reading, I returned to the pages that describe the production of chocolate chips, which have four numbered photographs on them. I asked, "What do fifty-eight thousand chocolate chips look like?"

One student said, "It would be a really big bag."

I narrowed the question: "If the chocolate chips were lined up or went around something, what might that look like?"

Angela said, "I think it might go around this room."

"It could maybe go all the way down the hallway," Damon added.

"I think they might be as long as the building," Casey suggested.

Several other students offered suggestions. I explained, "Today you are going find out what fifty-eight thousand chocolate chips might surround and what they might cover and then report back to the class."

I asked what the math terms were for *surround* and for *cover*. Students called out "perimeter" and "area." I then asked students to rephrase what their job was going to be today, using the math vocabulary. Several students volunteered and said that they would be finding the perimeter of a shape that could be outlined with fifty-eight thousand chocolate chips or the area of a shape that could be covered with that number of chocolate chips. I asked what shapes might work for their investigation. Students named various polygons and a circle.

I said to the class, "Now, if you tell me fifty-eight thousand chocolate chips would go around a rectangle that is one thousand inches by five hundred inches, I still won't know what that looks like. Once you measure, you need to have a way to tell me what that looks like—give me a real object or space that I can visualize." With that, I held up a small bag of Kissables and asked students to use these candies and any tools they needed to conduct the investigation. (Kissables, made by Hershey, are slightly larger than chocolate chips, and they are candy coated like M&M's, so they don't melt when students are handling them. In addition, their base measures about 1 centimeter in diameter, so they are a good manipulative for doing measurement conversions.)

Exploring the Problem

Day 1

I distributed the bags of candy and the *Chipping Away at Chocolate Chips* record sheets. Students worked in groups of four. Several groups started by trying to figure out how many Kissables would be in a foot. They came up with an estimate and then multiplied by three to find how many Kissables would be in a yard. Using proportions, they determined the number of yards long a line of fifty-eight thousand candies would be and recorded their answer. These groups naturally wanted to use a football field to visualize the perimeter because it was measured in yards. Some groups included the end zone; others didn't. One group recorded the width of the football field at 20 yards. When asked if this seemed reasonable, the group debated and then erased it. One student knew the width. In another group, one student looked up the exact dimensions of a standard field on a website (160 feet by 360 feet or 53 yards by 120 yards), including the end zones. (See Figure 2–1.)

Another group began to explore with centimeters after one student pointed out that this unit would be easier to use with a calculator. The group estimated a Kissable at 1.2 cm and multiplied by 58,000 to get 69,600 centimeters. The students figured out that this was 696 meters, approximately 700, and then decided they needed to measure the hallway.

Part I: One Minute of Chocolate Chips
58,000 thousand chocolate chips are made in just one minute!
What does this look like?
Explore with your special chocolate chips in two ways:

Foot‌ball Feild (s)

Perimeter → 1. What could 58,000 chocolate chips surround? Be sure your answer is
an object that is familiar to the rest of us. Show your work.

1 Kissable = 1 cm
30 Kissables = 1 ft (30 cm)
58,000 cm = 1,933.88 ft

Square = 58,000 ÷ 4 = 483.33 ft × 483.33
(14499.9 cm) × (14499.9 cm)

2 Football fields = 1 Square   27,000 kissables covers a football field
                                      (not including the inzones)
58000 ÷ 27000 = 2.14

2.14 football fields could be covered
by 58,000 kissables not including the inzones.

Figure 2–1: This group determined that the candies would equal the perimeter of 2.14 football fields.

Other groups picked classroom objects to use as visual images. One group measured the perimeter of the classroom; assuming it was square, they measured just one length. Another group measured a desktop, which was relatively square. Once they found the length around the desk, the students divided it by the length of the Kissable and found that it would take 206 candies to surround one desk, and therefore, 58,000 Kissables could surround about 281 desks. I asked them to take the next step and share what this meant in terms of how many classrooms would be needed to have 281 desks. A third group measured piece of paper and found that the Kissables could surround more than a ream of paper! (See Figures 2–2 through 2–4.)

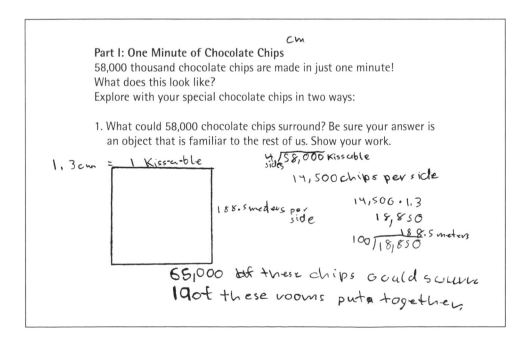

cm

Part I: One Minute of Chocolate Chips
58,000 thousand chocolate chips are made in just one minute!
What does this look like?
Explore with your special chocolate chips in two ways:

1. What could 58,000 chocolate chips surround? Be sure your answer is
an object that is familiar to the rest of us. Show your work.

1. 3 cm = 1 Kiss-a-ble

4 √58,000 Kissable
sides
14,500 chips per side

188.5 meters per side

14,506 · 1.3
18,850
100 √18,850 → 188.5 meters

65,000 of these chips could surround
19 of these rooms put a together.

Figure 2–2: This group compared the Kissables with the perimeter of our classroom.

Figure 2–3: These students
found that the candies
could surround 281.5 desks.

Part I: One Minute of Chocolate Chips
58,000 thousand chocolate chips are made in just one minute!
What does this look like?
Explore with your special chocolate chips in two ways:

1. What could 58,000 chocolate chips surround? Be sure your answer is
   an object that is familiar to the rest of us. Show your work.

1=1cm 58,000 cm.

perimeter of desk = 206 cm
we got this because the desk is 44 x 59

44
44
59
+59
206 cm

58000 ÷ 206 = 281.5.
58000 chocolate chips looks like this: If you put
chocolate chips side by side, like this
you would need 281½ desks to   DESK
hold 58000 chocolate chips if you
lined them up around the perimeter of the desk.

Figure 2–4: This group
explored the perimeter
of a piece of paper.

Part I: One Minute of Chocolate Chips
58,000 thousand chocolate chips are made in just one minute!
What does this look like?
Explore with your special chocolate chips in two ways:

1. What could 58,000 chocolate chips surround? Be sure your answer is
   an object that is familiar to the rest of us. Show your work.

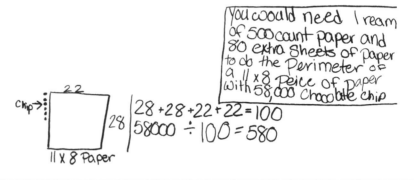

You would need 1 ream
of 500 count paper and
80 extra sheets of paper
to do the perimeter of
a 11 x 8 peice of paper
with 58,000 chocolate chip

chip→
22
28
11 X 8 Paper

28 + 28 + 22 + 22 = 100
58000 ÷ 100 = 580

When groups began working on area, many were troubled. In one
group the following discussion occurred:

"Let's figure out how many Kissables would be in the football
field."

"Well, we know that there are thirty in a foot, so in a square foot
there would be thirty times thirty, right?"

"Are you sure? Let's see." The student took the Kissables and
started making rows of thirty candies. "OK, I see, there would be nine
hundred. That seems like a lot."

"Right, so now if we multiply by three, we can find out how many
yards."

I could see that no one saw the error in this strategy, so I asked,
"Why did you multiply by three?"

Enrique said, "Because there are three feet in a yard."

"Are there three square feet in a square yard?" I asked. The group wasn't sure what I was asking. I explained, "You have said here that nine hundred kisses cover a square foot, right? So now you are trying to figure out how many of those square feet it takes to cover a square yard. Draw yourself a picture and report back to me how many square feet fill a square yard."

I later returned to the group.

"Nine—it takes nine square feet," one of the students reported.

"How did you figure that out?" I asked.

Mindy explained that they used grid paper and drew a representation of a square yard and they could see nine squares inside it.

I asked, "Then how does this help you figure out what fifty-eight thousand chips will cover?"

"Well, we figured out how many in a square yard, which is ninety Kissables by ninety Kissables, so we knew that it would be eight thousand one hundred Kissables in a square yard. Then we got a little more than seven [square] yards. We saw that in one ten-yard section of the field, it measures ten yards by fifty-three yards, so we figured the Kissables would cover just a small corner of the field."

One group wanted to use reams of paper for this part of the investigation. The students found the area of the paper in centimeters, estimating that a Kissable covered about 1 square centimeter. From there, they figured out the Kissables would cover ninety-five pieces of paper. (See Figure 2–5.) The group was surprised at this finding, given that the candies covered more than a ream of paper when surrounding the perimeter.

Students were very creative in choosing objects to measure and worked hard to figure out how to measure the area. Some finished, but some did not. Since not everyone was done and not much time was left in the period, I decided to delay sharing the results. Instead, I asked students to turn in their work and I saved it for the next day.

---

2. What could 58,000 chips cover? Be sure your answer is an object that is familiar to the rest of us. Show your work.

$22 \cdot 28 = 616$
$58000 \div 616 = 94.1 = 95$ Piece of Paper

you would need only 95 8x11 Piece of Paper to cover with 58,000 chips

Figure 2–5: This group explained how Kissables would cover ninety-five pieces of paper.

Figure 2–6: This group used proportions to solve the problem.

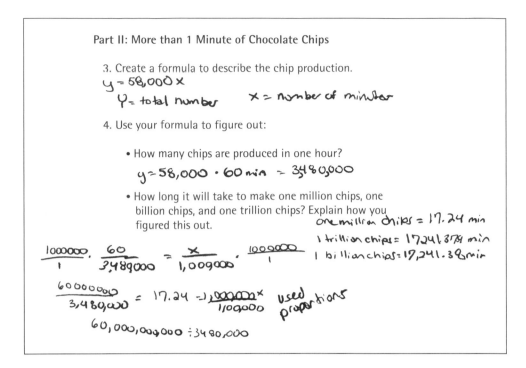

Part II: More than 1 Minute of Chocolate Chips

3. Create a formula to describe the chip production.
$y = 58,000 x$
Y = total number x = number of minutes

4. Use your formula to figure out:

• How many chips are produced in one hour?
$y = 58,000 \cdot 60 \text{ min} = 3,480,000$

• How long it will take to make one million chips, one billion chips, and one trillion chips? Explain how you figured this out.

one million chips = 17.24 min
1 trillion chips = 17,241,379 min
1 billion chips = 17,241.38 min

$\dfrac{1000000}{1} \cdot \dfrac{60}{3,480000} = \dfrac{x}{1,000000} \cdot \dfrac{1000000}{1}$

$\dfrac{60000000}{3,480,000} = 17.24 = \dfrac{1,000000 x}{1,000000}$ used proportions

$60,000,000,000 \div 3,480,000$

Day 2

As students arrived the next day, I explained that they needed to complete their perimeter and area illustrations of Kissables and work on the mathematical modeling for describing the production of chocolate chips (Part 2 of the investigation). Students worked in the same groups and had no trouble determining the formula: $t = 58,000m$ or $y = 58,000x$, where t or y is the number of chips and m or x is the number of minutes. They also had no trouble figuring out that they needed to multiply by 60 to figure out how many chips would be made in an hour (3,480,000 chips per hour).

Students used two different approaches to explore how many chips were produced in an hour and how long it would take to produce a million, a billion, and, finally, a trillion chips. (See Figures 2–6 and 2–7.) I explained to students that if they had time, they could try explaining what the billion chips would look like. (See Figure 2–8.)

I asked students to share their findings with the class. Each group prepared a presentation in which all group members had to contribute. Each group reported on the tools it used to solve the problem, what it found for the perimeter and area, and how it found them. Students were excited to share what they had done.

Additional Lesson Ideas

After they finished reading excerpts from the book *Chocolate,* students were more aware of the wide range of chocolate treats that are available today. It is a natural link to think about combining ingredients in

Figure 2–7: This group used division to solve the problem.

Part II: More than 1 Minute of Chocolate Chips

3. Create a formula to describe the chip production.

$C = m \cdot 58,000$ (C=chips M= minutes)

4. Use your formula to figure out:

- How many chips are produced in one hour?

$60 \cdot 58,000 = 3,480,000$ chips

- How long it will take to make one million chips, one billion chips, and one trillion chips? Explain how you figured this out.

$1,000,000 \div 58,000 = 17.24$ minutes

$1,000,000,000 \div 58000 = 17241.37$ minute or 287.35 hours

$1,000,000,000,000 \div 58000 = 17241379.31$ or 287356.32 hours

Figure 2–8: This student explained what one billion chips would look like.

5. Using your answers to 1 and 2, what would 1 billion chips look like? Explain (in words and/or pictures).

158400 m in a mile

249000 miles from the earth to the moon
5280 ft. in a mile
$5280 \cdot 240,000 = 1267200000 = $ feet from the moon
30 cm in a foot.
Multiply 1267200000 by 30 = 38,016,000,000 cm between the earth & the moon.

1 billion chocolate chips looks like $\frac{1}{38}$ of the distance from the earth to the moon.

1 billion cm

different ways to make a variety of chocolate candy bars. Here are some probability and combination ideas.

Candy Bar Attributes

- Types of Chocolate: dark chocolate, milk chocolate, white chocolate

- Nuts or no nuts

- Shapes: circle, oval, square, rectangle

- Fillings: vanilla cream, coconut cream, chocolate cream, orange cream, raspberry parfait, caramel, jelly, molasses chew, nougat, toffee

1. If each attribute above was represented in equal numbers in a collection of x number of candy bars, what is the probability that you would select the following?
   - a dark chocolate candy bar

- a chocolate candy bar with nuts
- a chocolate candy bar in the shape of a rectangle
- a chocolate candy bar with vanilla cream filling

2. Find the number of candy bars possible using two attributes.
   - How many different combinations are possible using all the types of chocolate and all the shapes?
   - How many different combinations of fillings and shapes are possible?
   - If all the types of chocolate are mixed with all the fillings, how many different candy bars can be made?

3. Find the number of candy bars possible using three attributes. How many different combinations are possible using all types of chocolate, all shapes, and nuts or no nuts?

4. Find the number of candy bars possible using four attributes. How many different candy bar combinations are possible using all types of chocolate, all shapes, nuts or no nuts, and all fillings?

Show students how making lists and tree diagrams are strategies that can help them find all the possible combinations. Also, some students may discover shortcuts for finding the possible combinations, such as multiplying 3×4 when using types of chocolate and shapes.

For additional statistics from the Chocolate Manufacturers Association, refer to the following websites: www.chocolateusa.org/Resources/statistical-information.asp and www.chocolateusa.org.

Cubes, Cones, Cylinders, and Spheres

Tana Hoban's picture book *Cubes, Cones, Cylinders, and Spheres* (2000) provides illustrations of shapes as they appear in real life. This book is full of beautiful photographs of real objects in the shapes of cubes, cones, cylinders, and spheres. Because these photographs are two-dimensional pictures of three-dimensional objects, they offer an excellent opportunity to explore the relationship between the two.

In this geometry investigation, students identify and name space shapes, meaning three-dimensional solid shapes, based on the characteristics of the shapes. Students also build a model of a space shape using connecting cubes and then make face-view drawings and isometric drawings of their model.

MATERIALS

multilink connecting cubes, at least 10 per student

square dot paper, 1 sheet per student (see Blackline Masters)

isometric dot paper, 1 sheet per student (see Blackline Masters)

an assortment of old magazines and newspapers

Introducing the Investigation

I began by showing the class pictures in the book *Cubes, Cones, Cylinders, and Spheres*. I asked students to name an object that they saw and a space shape that it resembled. After discussing the shapes in the book, we discussed the characteristics of space shapes. To prompt discussion, I asked the following questions:

- What do cylinders and cones have in common?

- What do cylinders and prisms have in common?

- What do cylinders and spheres have in common?

- What shape is missing from the book? (pyramid)

- The book has mostly cubes and rectangular prisms; what other kinds of prisms do you know? (triangular, hexagonal, and so on)

- How do specific kinds of pyramids and prisms get their name? (by the shape of the base)

- What do pyramids and prisms have in common?

- What do pyramids and cones have in common?

A Class Activity

After discussing the characteristics of space shapes, we talked about ways to draw pictures of three-dimensional shapes. We decided that we could draw a shape from one perspective at a time. In other words, we could draw what it looked like from the front, then from the top, and then from the side. Architects do this when they draw a house from three perspectives.

We also discussed drawing from all three perspectives at once, as in the photographs in the book. For example, the cube on the first page with the letter T on the top is drawn from the top, front, right corner. The cube with the letter C is drawn from the top, front, left corner. The cube with the 8 is drawn from the top, back, right corner. I then had them focus on the front cover of the book. These boxes are intended to be cubes. I asked, "What shape is each face of the cube?"

The students answered, "Square," without hesitation.

Then I asked, "When the box is drawn from the top, front, right perspective, are the faces drawn as squares?"

"They are actually diamonds or, what's the name? Oh yeah, rhombuses," answered Phil.

"Why are they drawn that way?" I asked.

"Because the squares have to be angled so that you can see more than one, which makes them look like they have angles other than ninety degrees," Melissa responded.

I turned to the page with the castle built from sugar cubes and asked the students from what perspective was this pictured. They responded that it was shown from the top, front, left perspective. I told them that they were each going to use the multilink connecting cubes to build their own three-dimensional model using approximately ten cubes; a few more or a few less was fine. I told them to keep their design private because they were going to make drawings of it and then someone else was going to have to use their drawings to reconstruct their model. I instructed the students to draw "face views" of their model, that is, the front of their model, the top of their model, and the right side of their model, on square dot paper. (Because we were looking at only one face at a time, we could draw the face view of the cube model using squares. See Figure 3–1.) I then asked them to draw their model from the top, front, right perspective on isometric dot paper. (See Figure 3–2.) I had them keep their model intact but hidden from the view of their classmates by using a binder or a folder.

I then collected the drawings, mixed them up, and passed them out so that each student had a set of drawings other than her own. I asked them to use only the face views at first to try to build the model. If they struggled with this or if they wanted to check what they had built, I told them to look at the isometric drawing. When they were done, I had them check with the builder to see if they had constructed the model appropriately and that it was a match for the original.

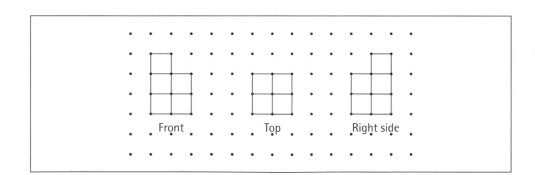

Figure 3–1: A replication of one student's face views drawn on square dot paper.

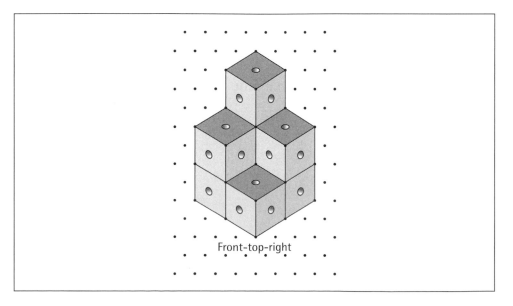

Figure 3–2: A replication of the same student's perspective view drawn on isometric dot paper.

Cubes, Cones, Cylinders, and Spheres

A Class Discussion

The class ended with a discussion of the advantages and disadvantages of each type of drawing. First I asked, "Which was easier to draw?"

Mia answered, "I think the face views are easier to draw. I get confused trying to make the isometric drawing because it is hard to picture the top and sides and I keep wanting to draw them like squares." Students continued to discuss their strategies for making isometric drawings.

Then I asked, "Which was easier to use to build?"

Josh replied, "It is easier to build the model looking at the isometric drawing. When you try to build using the face views, you have to keep adding blocks and moving them around because you build from one face at a time."

"Is it possible to use all the information in the pictures and still not build the model correctly?" I probed.

"Yes, because sometimes some of the blocks are hidden and they are not in any of the drawings. So you don't know if they are really there or not," answered Lindsay.

"Did anyone make a model that has the hidden cubes that Lindsay is talking about?" I asked.

Several students raised their hands and shared their models as well as the cubes in their models that were hidden or missing. An isometric drawing of a model with hidden missing cubes is shown in Figure 3–3.

Figure 3–3: Isometric drawing of a model with hidden missing cube.

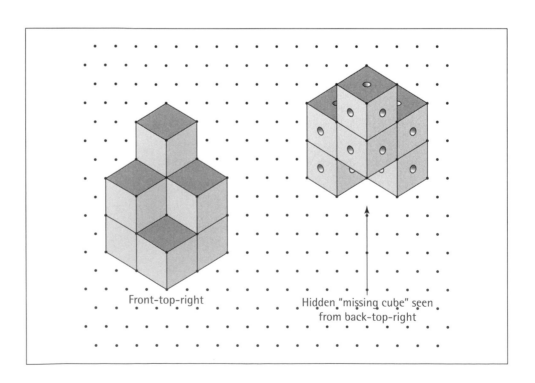

Front-top-right

Hidden "missing cube" seen from back-top-right

A Follow-Up Task

Students returned their materials, and I gave them a homework assignment. I told the students to look through newspapers and old magazines to find and cut out a picture that contained one or more of the shapes we'd been talking about. For each object in the picture they chose, they were to write a description that included the space shape it represented, the perspective it was drawn or pictured from, and the shape of the faces that could be seen in the picture. I had extra old magazines and newspapers available for students who didn't have access to them at home.

Everybody Loves Ice Cream

The Whole Scoop on America's Favorite Treat

Shannon Jackson Arnold's fact-filled book *Everybody Loves Ice Cream* (2004) has everything you would want to know about ice cream—from its history to its influence on American culture; from how to make great ice cream to the best places to buy it. Beautiful photographs enhance every page. This is a great book for an ice-cream lover to own and a fun book to share in middle school.

One section, "A Nation of Coneheads," tells the history of different kinds of cones. In this lesson, which focuses on patterns and algebra, students measure how tall one cone is, how tall two cones are, and so on, in order to predict the height of one hundred cones for two different kinds of cones. For each kind, they graph their data and find an equation to describe the height of any size stack of ice-cream cones.

MATERIALS

2-by-2-inch sticky notes, 1 per student

rulers marked in centimeters and/or meter sticks, 1 per small group of students

ice-cream cones, at least two different kinds such as sugar cones, cake cones, or jumbo cake cones, about 6 of one kind per small group of students

Everybody Loves Ice Cream **record sheets,** 1 per student (see Blackline Masters)

centimeter grid paper, 1 sheet per student (see Blackline Masters)

Introducing the Investigation

At the start of class, I asked each student to write his or her favorite ice-cream flavor on a sticky note and stick it to the board. When everyone was ready, I asked what the students noticed about their class favorites. Then I asked, "What are your favorite cones?"

"I like the waffle cones," Cassie said.

"Me, too," added Mindy and Andrew.

Jason disagreed. "I think the sugar cones taste better."

I showed students *Everybody Loves Ice Cream* and began reading "What's Your Flavor Profile?" on page 56, which briefly describes the personalities that match different flavors. I also read page 60, about the most popular flavors, before focusing on the cones themselves. For that, I read "1900s: A Cornucopia of Cones" on pages 19 and 20 and then "A Nation of Coneheads" on pages 117 through 121.

When I finished reading, I pointed to the picture of the cone holder on page 118 and asked the students how many cones they thought it might hold.

Zach said, "I think there will be fifty; that's how they sell them."

"I don't think that many would fit in there because they don't overlap as much as cups," Amber said questioningly.

"It would depend on the type of cone," began Meghan. "If they are the ones they have at the grocery store, it won't fit that many because they have that wide part at the top, but if they were those pointy cones, they don't have that wide part, so they might fit a lot more in there."

"Anything else that might influence how many cones fit?" I probed.

After a brief silence, Cody said excitedly, "How tall each cone is?"

To summarize, I said, "So, let's see, you have all suggested some ideas of what affects how many cones might be in this container. Raise your hand if you can remember what those things might be." Several students summarized that the shape and the height of the cone could make a difference. With that we put the book down and moved to the investigation.

A Class Activity

I gave each group a meter stick and a stack of identical ice-cream cones—some groups had sugar, some had waffle, and some had cake cones—and gave each student a record sheet. To begin, I asked the class to predict how tall one hundred cones would be. There was a wide range of predictions.

Next I asked each student to complete the table on the record sheet with measurements for one through ten cones for their stack of cones. The students stacked their cones one at a time and measured the new

Figure 4–1: This student found a pattern when measuring cake cones.

1. What is your prediction? *2 meters*

2. Complete the table for your stack of cones.

Kind of cone: _small cake cone (Kroger)_

Number of Cones	Height of Stack (to the nearest tenth of a cm)
1	7 cm
2	9½ cm
3	12 cm
4	14½ cm
5	17 cm
6	19½ cm
7	22
8	24½
9	27
10	29½
20	54.5
30	79.5
40	104.5
50	129.5

3. If you continue with this pattern, how tall would a stack of 100 cones be? Explain how you determined this.

I think it would be 254½ cm cuz every cone would add only 2.5cm cuz the bottom part is inside the other cone so I did 50×25 to add it to the other 50 cones

4. How close was your prediction to the actual height of the stack?

Pretty close by only 54½ cm

height of the stack, using a meter stick, to the nearest tenth of a centimeter. The sugar cone was the easiest to work with because the stack grew 2 centimeters each time a cone was added to it. The cake cones were more difficult in terms of finding a pattern. (See Figure 4–1.) In fact, some students didn't think there was a pattern at all.

Looking at her table, Melissa noted, "There isn't a pattern with these cones."

"Look at your stack of cones," I suggested, "and consider whether you think there should be a pattern."

Nate said, "If you look at the numbers, they aren't increasing the same each time."

Again, I suggested they look at the stack of cones.

Math and Nonfiction, Grades 6–8

"Oh, wait, each time the only part of the cone we can see is the wide part," Melissa said as she pointed eagerly at the stack, lifting a cone in and out of it.

"So, if that is the only part, then it should be the same each time," reasoned Charlene.

"So, let's recheck our measurements," Melissa suggested.

After reviewing their measurements, the group agreed that the growth was about the same amount every time, with maybe some slight differences because of some chips in the cones.

I asked, "How can you figure out how much the stack increases every time?"

Charlene suggested, "If we subtract the [new] height from the height of the stack before it is added, we would get the increase."

"So, we just subtract each one of these to see if they are the same, right?" Nate clarified.

"If it is off," Melissa continued, "then we probably have a measuring error, so we can fix it."

When they didn't get the same amount each time, they went back and measured again and found some small measuring inaccuracies.

Once the groups had completed their tables for ten cones, I asked them to complete the table for twenty, thirty, forty, and fifty cones. This proved to be somewhat challenging. Some students wanted to double the amount for ten to get twenty. To illustrate that this would not work, I took a stack of about seven cones and held it up. Then I took a second stack about the same height and asked, "If I measured these two stacks separately and then added the two heights, would that be the same as one stack with all of these cones?" As I was talking, I joined the two stacks into one.

"No," said a number of students.

"It's not the same," Darren stated, "because you lose the bottom of the one cone."

"Right," Raymond agreed. "See, when you have two stacks, you have two full cones, and when you combine them, you can only see one full cone."

"What does that mean, then, for your tables when you are finding the height for twenty, thirty, forty, and fifty cones?" I asked.

"That we can't just double ten to get twenty or fifteen to get thirty," Sara replied.

Students returned to the task. The students with the sugar cones figured out a solution the fastest. They said they would add 20 centimeters to the height of ten cones because they were adding ten more cones and each cone added 2 centimeters to the height of the stack. Using this ratio of 20 centimeters per ten cones, they continued adding 20 centimeters to get the height for thirty, forty, fifty, and even one hundred cones.

The groups with other types of cones found the task somewhat harder. One group found the height of their stack of cones grew about 2.7 centimeters each time they stacked on another cone. They multiplied 2.7 by 10 and got 27 centimeters for every ten cones. Like the previous group, they added 27 centimeters to the height of ten cones to get the height of twenty cones. They continued to add 27 centimeters to find the height of thirty, forty, fifty, and one hundred cones.

Most students were surprised when they compared the estimated heights with their predictions because the stacks were taller than they had anticipated. We talked about things in the room that were about the height of their stacks to give them a reference point.

Next, I distributed centimeter grid paper and asked the students to graph their data and then determine if their pattern was linear or nonlinear. They did this with little difficulty and were able to identify all the patterns as linear. I noticed that as students were working, many of them were connecting their points with a line. I asked, "What does it mean when you connect the points with a line?"

After a pause, I asked the question a different way. "Select a new point that is not in your table but is on the line, and point to it."

I waited and then asked, "I want you to record that coordinate pair and then talk to your group about what that pair means for this situation."

After giving groups time to debate this issue, I asked the class, "What does the point tell us?"

"It says that for five and a half cones, the height would be about fifteen centimeters," Diedre offered, "but that won't work."

"You can't have a half of cone," several students said at once.

I asked, "What does that mean for your graphs?"

"That we shouldn't connect the points because there are no answers between them."

"Yes," I agreed. "This is called a *discrete function* because it is a function only for certain values of x and y. We have looked at many functions that are continuous, but this one is not continuous; it is discrete."

Finally, I asked students to write a rule for calculating the height of a stack of any number of cones of the kind they were using. We had been working with equations in the form $y = a + bx$, so we discussed how to use this form of equation to write a rule. Many students wanted to use the height of the first cone for a. However, when I asked them how to find the y-intercept or starting value in the table, they answered that x had to be zero. Since zero cones would have a height of zero, they were stuck. We changed directions for a minute and focused on b. This was fairly simple because they had been doing work with the rate of change already.

I asked the students what b represents.

"Slope," answered one student.

"Rate of change," answered another.

"Does anyone remember how we calculate or determine what b is?" I asked.

"It's the change in y over the change in x," replied a student.

"In this case, what is it?" I asked.

"Change in height of the stack of cones over the change in the number of cones," answered a student.

"What does the change in height actually depend on? Yes, the number of cones, but what part of the cone specifically? Think about how the stack of cones looks," I replied.

"The rim of the cone," answered a student.

"So b is the height of the rim or lip of the cone because that's what changes the height each time you add a cone to the stack. The *hold* of the cone, where you wrap your hand around to hold the cone, goes inside the stack and doesn't appear to affect the height of the stack," I confirmed.

We returned to the idea of zero cones. According to their graphs, if they continued their patterns "down one" from the coordinates for one cone, they would hit the y-axis at about 5 centimeters or 8 centimeters, depending on which cone they were using. Technically that meant that if they had zero cones, they would still have a height of 5 or 8 centimeters. If they put a point at $(0, 0)$, however, the points wouldn't all line up, as they would expect in a linear situation.

I said to the class, "You just explained to me the rate of change was the height of each lip. So, think about how to explain the point on the y-axis, using the notion that your formula describes the number of lips, rather than the number of cones," I suggested.

After some wait time, a number of hands were raised.

Tonya said, "The point on the y-axis means zero rims, the height when you have zero rims."

"It's like if you cut the cone off right here," Melissa pointed, "and all you had left is the one cone's bottom part; that is what you have—zero tops."

"It's the base of the cone, just the base," Kanisha summarized.

We decided to use the number of lips instead of the number of cones as the label on the x-axis so that we could see the y-intercept on the graphs. The groups went back to work. Again, this was easiest for the groups with the sugar cones because they could easily see that they could work backward by subtracting 2 centimeters for each cone to get to $x = 0$ lips. (See Figures 4–2 and 4–3.)

Having the cones available as concrete tools was effective in helping students reason about concepts that were difficult for them, including discrete functions, measuring accurately, and determining

Figure 4–2: Students graphed their data and used the graph to determine if their pattern was linear or nonlinear.

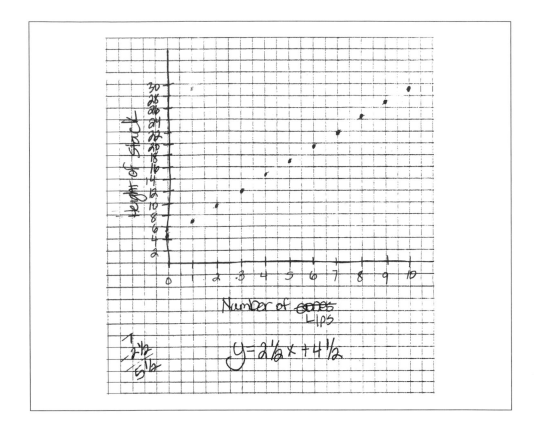

Figure 4–3: This illustration shows how $y = a + bx$ applied to stacking cones.

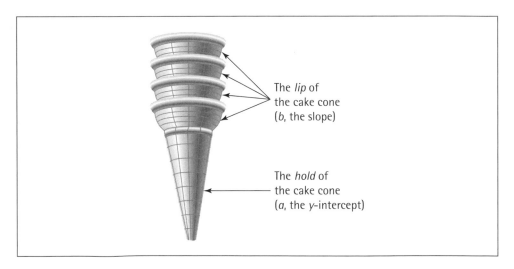

The *lip* of the cake cone (*b*, the slope)

The *hold* of the cake cone (*a*, the *y*-intercept)

an equation from a table or a graph. The context of this problem enabled students to move between representations and better understand each representation. At the end of the lesson, one student remarked, "We never knew how much math was used to figure out how to box up ice-cream cones!"

Math and Nonfiction, Grades 6-8

Fantastic Feats and Failures

Fantastic Feats and Failures, by the editors of *Yes Mag* (2004), is a collection of stories about engineering successes and failures. It explains how buildings, bridges, towers, vehicles, and more were designed and built. We marvel at the feats, but the failures teach valuable lessons.

The focus of this investigation is the Citicorp Building in New York City. The geometric design of support columns allowed this building to be constructed on stilts. Students select one feature of a column, for example, its width, and explore how variance in that measure would affect the strength of the column. The mathematics of this lesson includes data collection and analysis, designing an experiment, and measuring accurately.

MATERIALS

paperback books, thin and all having identical heights, about 100 (see page 34)

rulers, 1 per small group of students

a computer or graphing calculator to display data for the class

optional: 11-by-17 inch blank paper, several sheets per small group of students

Introducing the Investigation

You may want to read the entire book to the class or only parts of it. For this lesson, I selected several feats and failures from the twenty described. After reading about them, I focused on the Citicorp Building, described on pages 22–23.

The class and I discussed the project's successes and failures. Engineers were able to successfully design the building so it would fit in the "air space" above the church that owned the land. Stilts made the building possible, but engineers still had to overcome some challenges, such as the sway of the structure. The failure of this building was not in the design but in the construction. A change was made that caused the building to be too weak to withstand strong winds, and the hurricane season was on its way! Fortunately, the engineers came to the rescue and were able to find a way to compensate for the weakness in the building's construction. The building is now a familiar feature of the Manhattan skyline and is an example of an engineering feat.

On the board, I sketched a flowchart of the successes and failures of the building with the students' help. Then we focused on the columns. Since there is not much discussion in the book about the columns that enabled the skyscraper to be built in the air, this became the focus of our math lesson.

I asked the class, "What factors do you think an engineer would have to consider in the design of the columns?"

"They had to consider where to put them. It said in the book that they had to be in the middle of the building," answered Brian.

I wrote *position* on the board and said, "OK, what else? Many of the considerations are probably not even discussed in the book."

"Maybe they had to think about the shape of the columns. I was thinking they would be round, but those look like rectangles," Ann replied. I wrote *shape* on the board.

Darren then suggested, "What about the height? I know they said ten stories, but how did they decide that? Could they have been taller?" I wrote *height* on the board.

"The width. Darren is talking about making them taller, but I think that they would be sturdier if they were wider," offered Karmen. I wrote *width* on the board.

"What about the material they used to build them?" Dalton wondered.

I wrote *building material* on the board and said, "You have made some great suggestions. Let's take some of these ideas and see if we can experiment with them to get some answers."

I explained that the students were going to work in groups to build columns from $8\frac{1}{2}$-by-11-inch paper, concentrating on changes to one of the characteristics listed on the board while leaving the others the same. I told them that they would stack identical paperback books on top of their columns, one at a time, until they collapsed and then record the number of books that the columns could hold. (I had borrowed from the school librarian several class sets of the same book that amounted to about one hundred books.)

Next I assigned each group of four an experimental variable. I wrote the words *height* and *width* two times each on separate slips of paper. I put the four slips of paper into a bowl and had the groups each draw one. Then I asked the groups to discuss how they were going to build their columns. When a group was able to describe its procedure to me, I allowed the students to get their materials (twenty-five books, twelve sheets of paper, scissors, tape, and a ruler). For the groups working with width, we discussed the issue of using diameter or circumference. Because circumference was easier to measure (they could unwrap the paper and get an accurate measure), students chose this as the way to measure width.

Observing the Students

As they designed their approaches to exploring the strength of the columns, I observed and questioned students.

Group 1

Group 1 was assigned height. The students decided to make round columns. They chose to use the paper to make all the columns the same height at first and then cut the columns to various heights after forming them so that they would all be created the same way. To make a really tall column, they used an 11-by-17-inch piece of paper. I asked them how they were going to control their variables if they used a different-size piece of paper. They said they were going to use the $8\frac{1}{2}$-by-11-inch piece of paper and roll it up "the long way" so that the tallest column they could make would be $8\frac{1}{2}$ inches. When they rolled it up, they would overlap the paper slightly so that they could tape the two ends together. Recognizing that one dimension of the two different-size pieces of paper shared the same length, they decided to roll the biggest piece of paper "the short way" so that they could make a column 17 inches tall, as you can see in the last row in the table in Figure 5–1. This way all of the columns would have the same width. I gave them the go-ahead and they got started.

Group 2

The second group, which was also investigating height, struggled to decide how to make the columns. The students' plan was to cut their pieces of paper to various heights and then roll them up and tape them. There was little consideration of overlap or consistency. I asked Group 1 and Group 2 to discuss their plans with each other and to check back with me when they were done. I felt this would get them started and would give me a chance to check on other groups. When I checked back in with Group 2, the students had a much better idea of how to construct

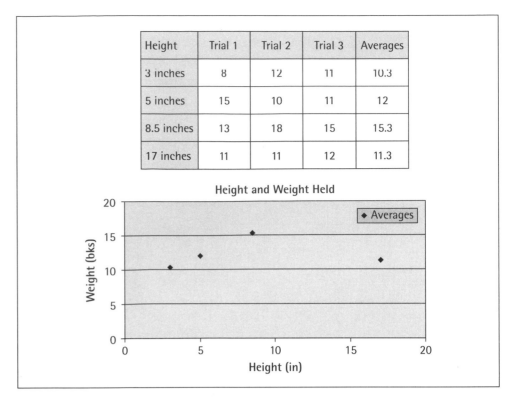

Figure 5–1: Group 1's table and graph, showing how changes in height affected how many books the column could hold.

Height	Trial 1	Trial 2	Trial 3	Averages
3 inches	8	12	11	10.3
5 inches	15	10	11	12
8.5 inches	13	18	15	15.3
17 inches	11	11	12	11.3

Height and Weight Held

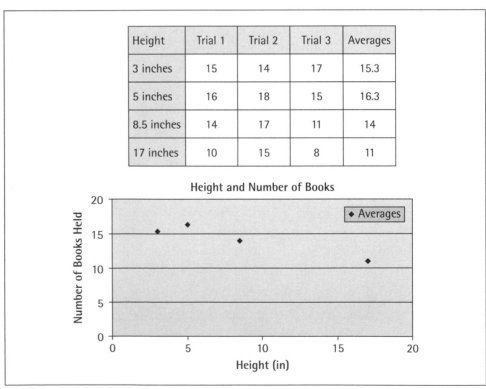

Figure 5–2: Group 2 investigated the same heights as Group 1 so the groups could compare their results.

Height	Trial 1	Trial 2	Trial 3	Averages
3 inches	15	14	17	15.3
5 inches	16	18	15	16.3
8.5 inches	14	17	11	14
17 inches	10	15	8	11

Height and Number of Books

their columns more accurately. They even used the same height measurements as Group 1 so that they could better compare their results in the end! This was not something I had thought of as they began the task, but I was impressed that they wanted to be "consistent." (See Figure 5–2.)

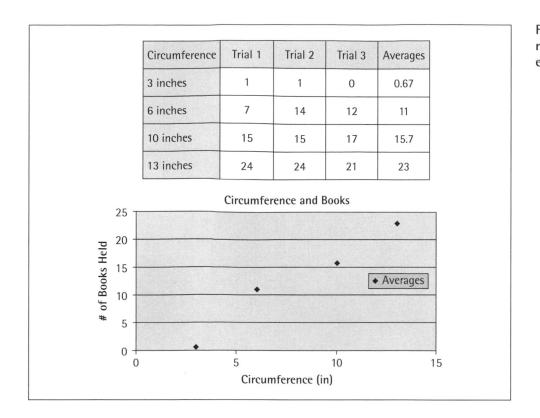

Figure 5–3: Group 3's results for the circumference investigation.

Circumference	Trial 1	Trial 2	Trial 3	Averages
3 inches	1	1	0	0.67
6 inches	7	14	12	11
10 inches	15	15	17	15.7
13 inches	24	24	21	23

Group 3

The third group was assigned width and was therefore exploring and measuring different options for the circumferences of the columns. As I approached the students, they had a piece of paper and were discussing where the circumference would be if it were rolled up as a column. One student then unrolled the column to show that the circumference was really the length of the paper. They decided to use the $8\frac{1}{2}$-inch side of the paper as the height of the column and cut various lengths to roll and form the circumferences of the columns. They appeared to be headed in the right direction, so I moved on to observe Group 4 while Group 3 finished its discussion. (See Figure 5–3.)

Group 4

Group 4 was having a similar discussion, but one student was trying to sketch a drawing of the circumference of the column, and it appeared that not everyone was able to picture what was being discussed. I suggested that the student use the paper to model what he was talking about. This seemed to clear up the confusion. I realized that Groups 3 and 4 were in a similar place and asked the two groups to share ideas about how they wanted to design the columns. Meanwhile I moved back to check on Group 2. After Group 2 suggested that it keep its measurements the same as Group 1's for consistency, I went back to Groups 3 and 4 and suggested they do the same. (See Figure 5–4.)

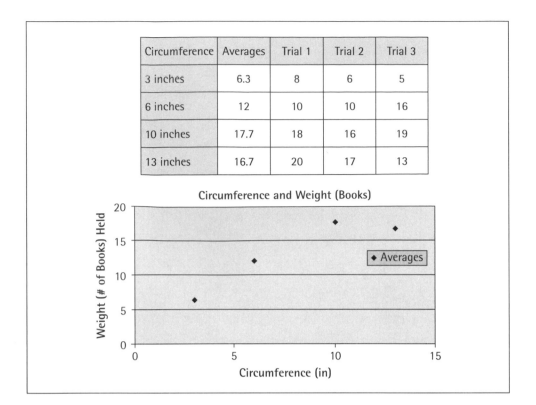

Figure 5–4: Group 4's table and graph for the circumference investigation.

Circumference	Averages	Trial 1	Trial 2	Trial 3
3 inches	6.3	8	6	5
6 inches	12	10	10	16
10 inches	17.7	18	16	19
13 inches	16.7	20	17	13

A Class Discussion

The following day, we went to the computer lab, where each group entered its data into an Excel document and made a scatter plot of the data. I saved the tables and graphs to my memory stick, and we returned to my classroom, where I then projected the tables and graphs so that the whole class could see them. (A graphing calculator can also be used for this part of the activity.)

Groups 1 and 2 shared their height data. I asked the class if there were any patterns in the data.

John noted, "Both groups have graphs that sort of go up and then down but not exactly the same."

"Can someone describe the graphs using the variables of height and strength?" I asked.

"Yes, the amount of books it can hold goes up when the height gets bigger at first, but then the number of books goes down when the height gets even bigger," answered Katie.

"Why do you think that is?" I asked.

Julie raised her hand and explained, "I think it starts to get sturdier at first but then when it gets too tall, it sort of bends in the middle and falls. Kind of like when you build with blocks as a kid. Eventually it is going to fall over!"

"Why do the graphs not look exactly the same even though you did things very much the same way?" I probed.

Dan answered, "It was really hard to do it exactly the same. I think that even in our own experiment, we didn't always use exactly the same amount of tape and sometimes people didn't put the books on the exact same way."

"So, do you think height is something an engineer needs to consider?"

Students answered in unison with "Yes" and "Definitely."

"OK, then," I went on. "How about Groups 3 and 4 with circumference?"

"It definitely looks like they keep going up," suggested Katie.

"Can someone describe the graph using the variables?" I asked. "Sam, I haven't heard from you yet. What do you think?"

"I think it shows that as the circumference gets bigger, it will hold more weight."

"Yeah, but eventually the books would fall inside the column!" Marty exclaimed.

"Not if the columns weren't hollow," replied Julie.

"So you would want to make the columns as wide as possible, but make sure to consider other things," Andy concluded.

"Based on our experiment, would circumference of the column be an important thing for an engineer to consider?" I asked.

Again, in unison students agreed.

"There are a number of things that we didn't include in our experiment that engineers would have to consider, but this gives you an idea of how complicated designing and building something can be. Hopefully you will look at all buildings a little differently now!" And with that, we ended the class.

Go Figure!
A Totally Cool Book About Numbers

Go Figure! by Johnny Ball (2005), has a wealth of interesting mathematical information sorted into four parts—"Where Do Numbers Come From?" "Magic Numbers," "Shaping Up," and "The World of Math." For example, the section "Take a Chance," in the last part, focuses on probability, explaining why casinos always win, offering ideas about "sneaky" spinners, and linking probability and pi. The intriguing, short two-page pieces, along with many beautiful illustrations, make this book a wonderful resource for students and a great opportunity to do a range of mathematics lessons.

"Mendel's Numbers," a discussion in "Take a Chance" on page 76, describes how Gregor Mendel discovered genes by combining purple and white flowering peas. Students connect to this idea by using tree diagrams and arrays to determine the probability of two independent events. Using these two visual representations allows students to see connections between the two ways to predict probability, builds connections to science, and accounts for different learning styles. Then they design an experiment to see how reality compares with probability and determine the frequency of genetic results for their experiment and then for the whole-class data. After investigating the flowering pea example, students explore the probability of being a tongue curler.

MATERIALS

Go Figure! record sheets, 1 per student (see Blackline Masters)

an assortment of manipulatives for investigating the probability of two independent events, such as the following:

dice, about 10

pairs of cards (one purple and one white card, or two different playing cards), about 5 pairs

spinners divided into either halves or fourths, about 5

coins, about 10

Note: This lesson was taught in a ninety-minute block but can be adapted to a two-day investigation with the experiment completed on Day 1 and the tongue-curling problems explored on Day 2.

Introducing the Investigation

I began the lesson by telling the class that I wanted to share some interesting facts from a book titled *Go Figure!* I first read the introductory paragraph to "Take a Chance" on page 76, which begins with "What's the chance of being struck by lightning . . . ," and then read "Risky Business" on page 77, including the probability of dying from different causes. I asked students which of the causes people were most likely to die from.

Several students said, "Smoking."

I asked which was the least likely cause of death, and many students called out, "Getting hit by a meteorite." I then asked students to compare the chance of getting killed by playing soccer with the chance of being murdered.

Amy said, "It's more likely to get killed playing soccer—that doesn't sound right."

Martel replied, "It's because soccer is played so much."

Louis asked if this information was true in our country or in the world.

I said, "Good point. This data is from Europe and North America, so maybe the statistics would look different if the data were from just the United States."

After students shared several other observations, I said, "What I want to read to you now explains how you look the way you do."

I read "Mendel's Numbers" on the bottom of page 76 aloud, then asked students if they had studied genes. Several students said that they had done so in science and were familiar with the genetics 2-by-2 table.

I said to the class, "I'd like you to think about tongue curling, but not try it yet. If you think it is likely that someone is a tongue curler, show a thumbs-up; if you think it is not likely, then show a thumbs-down." (I had to stop midway through the statement to remind the students not to show their tongues.) Once everyone had given a thumb prediction, I said, "OK, you can show your tongue—curl it if you can." Most of the students were able to curl their tongues.

I told them that tongue curling is a dominant trait: if a person has only one gene for tongue curling, she will still "show" tongue curling. I modeled the 2-by-2 table and the tree diagram techniques for finding the possible combinations of genes, using C for curl and N for no curl:

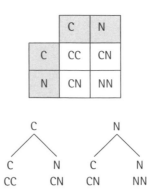

I asked students what it meant to have CN and if that person would be able to curl his tongue. I summarized by asking what the probability of being able to curl your tongue was if you had one parent who could and one who couldn't. About half of the students had their hands up at this point with stories to share of their own inherited traits and anomalies. Allysa said, "If both my parents can curl their tongues, then why can't I?"

This question allowed me to bring the personal stories to an end. I said, "Allysa has just asked the very question that we are going to explore today. By the end of the lesson, she will be able to answer her own question about how it might be possible for two parents with the same trait to produce a child with a different trait. Let's first look at the flowering pea problem that Mendel explored. I want you to use a tree diagram and a two-by-two table to show the possible combinations of the mixed-gene peas created from the purple peas and the white peas."

A Class Activity

I distributed the record sheets. I wrote on the board the genetic way to use variables, in this case P for purple and p for white (capital letters for the dominant trait and lowercase for the recessive). This confused students, so I modified this practice and allowed them to use P for purple and W for white.

Students worked independently for about five minutes, mostly using the 2-by-2 table to find out the possible outcomes. When they had finished, I asked them to share what they had found.

Estria said, "One-fourth would be white."

Remani said, "I got half."

I asked for elaboration and he replied, "The ones on the bottom row would be white—oh, wait, seventy-five percent—no, OK, twenty-five percent."

To be sure he was clear in his own thinking, I said, "Why do you now say twenty-five percent?"

"Because," Remani elaborated, "there are three that have a white gene, but only one that has two white, so it is the only one that looks white."

A few other students were not clear on how the table could be interpreted, so I asked them to take two minutes to share with their partners and convince each other of what the flower would show for each of the possible combinations.

Then I asked, "If you matched up two parents who each had one dominant and one recessive gene, would 25 percent of their children have the recessive trait? Let's say, for example, the flowers make twenty new flowers; write on your paper exactly how many of the flowers you think would be white."

Students recorded their answers and then I asked for volunteers to share.

Tamara replied, "I think there will be five white flowers because it is a twenty-five percent chance out of twenty flowers. Twenty-five percent of twenty is five."

"I knew that white-white was only one out of four and twenty divided by four is five," explained Nicolas.

"Does anyone have a different prediction?" I asked.

Mark said, "I think it could be six because you don't really know for sure."

From glancing at students' papers, I could see that they had all recorded five as their prediction. I said, "Well, we don't have time to breed flowers, but how might we design an experiment that could model the idea of selecting, at random, one of two genes from each parent?"

The class was quiet for a full minute, then Amanda timidly said, "Could we use spinners?" The class had used spinners earlier in the year in a probability unit.

"How might you use a spinner?" I probed.

Chara said, "If it was half and half, then if it lands on one side, then it would be purple and if it lands on the other, it would be white."

"Interesting," I said. "What do the rest of you think about that?"

Several students said, "Yeah, yes, that would work."

I said, "Any other tools we might use?"

"Cards," Tammy called out.

I pulled some white and purple cards out of my pocket. "You mean like these?" She smiled. "How would these be used?" I asked the students. They weren't sure. I picked one of each card and put them behind my back and walked up to Nina and asked her to pick my right or left hand. When she picked my right, I held up the white card.

Then I asked, "What does this show?"

Nicolas said, "It shows that from one parent you picked a white gene."

"So what do I need to do now?" I asked.

"Do it again," several students called out.

I asked one more time, "Are there other tools we could use?"

Allysa said, "Couldn't we use dice?"

"How would you use dice?" Andre asked.

After some silence, I offered, "Evens could be white and odds could be purple."

Carlitta said, "Oh yeah, and we could color one die purple and then it would show both parents."

Kelly asked, "Can we flip coins?" She wasn't sure what to do with the coins, but after thinking for a minute she concluded, "Oh yeah, we could do heads as purple and tails as white."

I instructed students to talk with their partners and decide which tool they wanted to use and to send up a representative to get that tool. Their job was to do their experiment twenty times. I had to clarify that an experiment included two events, meaning drawing a card twice, spinning a spinner twice, or rolling one die two times (or rolling two dice once). Students picked from the three ways to do the experiment so that at least two pairs were using each tool.

Observing the Students

As groups worked on their experiments, I noticed there was still some confusion about what the offspring would look like. So as I moved

Figure 6–1: This student used dice to investigate crossing two peas.

> 2. If you cross two peas that are mixed (Pp), what is the probability of getting a white-flowered pea?
>
> Prediction: __5__
> Design an experiment to see what actually happens after twenty trials.
>
> | Describe experiment here | | | | Record your data here |
> |---|---|---|---|---|
> | 1. PP | 6. PP | 11. Pw | 16. Pw | Purple = 16 |
> | 2. PP | 7. ww | 12. PP | 17. Pw | white = 4 |
> | 3. Pw | 8. ww | 13. PP | 18. PP | |
> | 4. Pw | 9. Pw | 14. ww | 19. ww | = dominant |
> | 5. PP | 10. Pw | 15. Pw | 20. Pw | = recessive |

2. If you cross two peas that are mixed (Pp), what is the probability of getting a white-flowered pea?

Prediction: __5__

Design an experiment to see what actually happens after twenty trials.

Describe experiment here	Record your data here
Purple PP 12 White ‖‖‖‖ 8 Pw | ww ‖‖‖‖‖‖ | ‖‖‖‖ ‖‖‖‖ |	We shuffled 2 Cards behind our Backs and picked at random. I didn't think we'd get so many whites

Figure 6–2: This student used cards to investigate crossing two peas.

from group to group, I asked students to tell me which of their results were turning out to be white and which were purple.

This experiment took about fifteen minutes (the card pullers took the longest). (See Figures 6–1 and 6–2.)

A Class Discussion

As soon as they were done, students recorded their events on a table on the board:

Our Class Data for Flowering Peas

Purple	White
16	4
15	5
16	4
16	4
15	5
10	10
17	3
16	4
12	8
14	6

Carlitta reached for her calculator and a few minutes later reported, "The averages are fourteen and seven-tenths for purple and five and three-tenths for white."

I said to the class, "Wow, how many of you got what you expected?" Only two groups' results matched the expected values of fifteen purple and five white. "How many of you got more white than you expected? More purple than you expected?"

Next I asked, "What does this experiment tell us about probability and about genetics?"

Kimberly said, "It's not exact; you aren't going to get what you should all the time."

"With our whole class we are a lot closer, but in our [partner] experiments, there is a much bigger range," Natalie observed. "So really, if you are only picking a few, you don't really know how it is going to turn out."

I said, "If the flower has four offspring, will one of them have white flowers and three have purple?"

Some students still thought that would happen; others argued that we really didn't know for sure—it was just possible.

Having established that we were talking only about what was likely, and not what was definite, we moved back to tongue curling.

"Let's investigate the tongue curling using capital and lowercase letter Ts like in biology," I said. "What if the mom could not curl her tongue [tt] and the dad could curl his tongue, but had one of each gene [Tt]? What is likely to happen with their children?"

Students worked in pairs to complete 2-by-2 tables. (See Figure 6–3.) When sharing, some students said they thought that 50 percent would show tongue curling. One student suggested 25 percent, but in relooking at his table, he realized he had just made a recording error.

I said to the class, "Recall that Alyssa has two parents who can curl their tongues, but she can't. What are her father's and mother's possible genes for tongue curling?"

I waited for students to think about it and several hands went up, including Alyssa's. I called on her and she said, "Both of my parents would have to have Tt—then they can curl and I ended up with tt—no curl."

Figure 6–3: This student used a 2-by-2 table to investigate tongue curling.

4. Show the theoretical probability of being a tongue curler if one parent isn't and the other is.

Math and Nonfiction, Grades 6–8

To push their thinking further, I asked the class to find all the possible parent combinations that would give a probability of zero (0 percent) for being a tongue curler and those that would give a probability of one (100 percent) for being a tongue curler. Students worked on this until there were only five minutes of class left. In the first case, there is only one way: if both parents are not tongue curlers (tt and tt). In the second case, there are two possibilities: Tt and TT or TT and TT. Some students found both ways; most found the latter way. (See Figures 6–4 and 6–5.) In the closing five minutes, I asked students to think about the genetics they had explored and the probability experiment they did and reflect in writing on what they had learned. (See Figures 6–6 through 6–11.)

Applying Your Knowledge
5. Under what conditions would the probability of producing a tongue curler be 0? Explain.

	t	t
t	tt	tt
t	tt	tt

If both parents couldn't curl their tongue and they had two recessive genes (tt).

Figure 6–4: One student's solution to the circumstances that had a probability of zero for being a tongue curler.

6. Under what conditions would the probability of producing a tongue curler be 1? Explain.

	T	T
T	TT	TT
+	T+	T+

The parents would have a Tt and the other parent can have a TT. Or both parents can have a TT.

Figure 6–5: One student's solution to the circumstances that had a probability of one for being a tongue curler.

7. For each prompt below, *write a paragraph related to your genetics exploration.*
What we found . . .

We found that the probability is what is most likely to happen, but since there is no certain way to tell, not all the results are perfect.

Figure 6–6: One student's insights about probability.

7. For each prompt below, *write a paragraph related to your genetics exploration.*
What we found . . .

Probability is always theoretical; Nothing is absolutly certain.

Figure 6–7: Another student's insights about probability.

Figure 6–8: One student explains what she learned about probability.

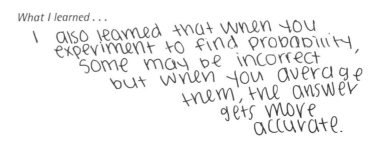

What I learned . . .

I also learned that when you experiment to find probability, some may be incorrect but when you average them, the answer gets more accurate.

Figure 6–9: A student's explanation of what she learned about genetics.

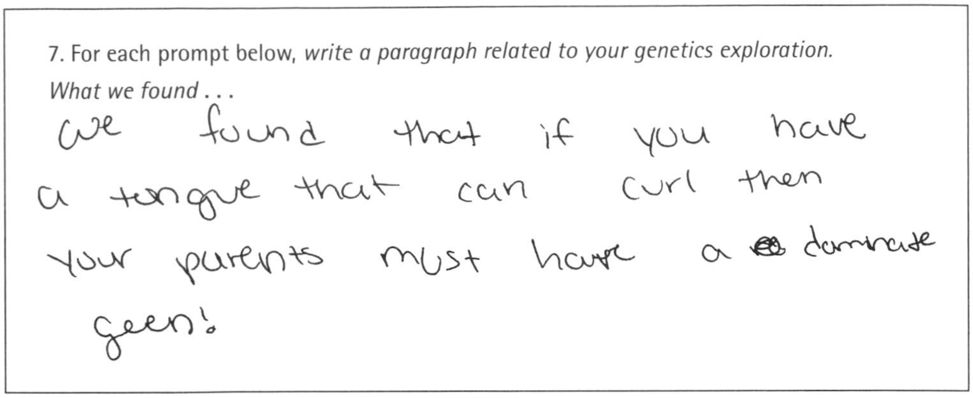

7. For each prompt below, *write a paragraph related to your genetics exploration.*

What we found . . .

We found that if you have a tongue that can curl then your parents must have a dominate geen!

Figure 6–10: Another student explained what she learned about genetics.

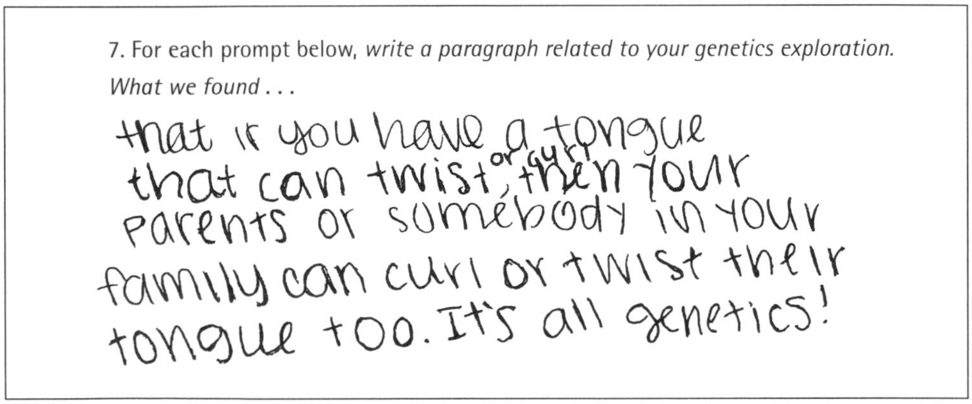

7. For each prompt below, *write a paragraph related to your genetics exploration.*

What we found . . .

that if you have a tongue that can twist or curl, then your parents or somebody in your family can curl or twist their tongue too. It's all genetics!

Figure 6–11: This student illustrated both techniques for finding genetics and the connection between genetics and probability.

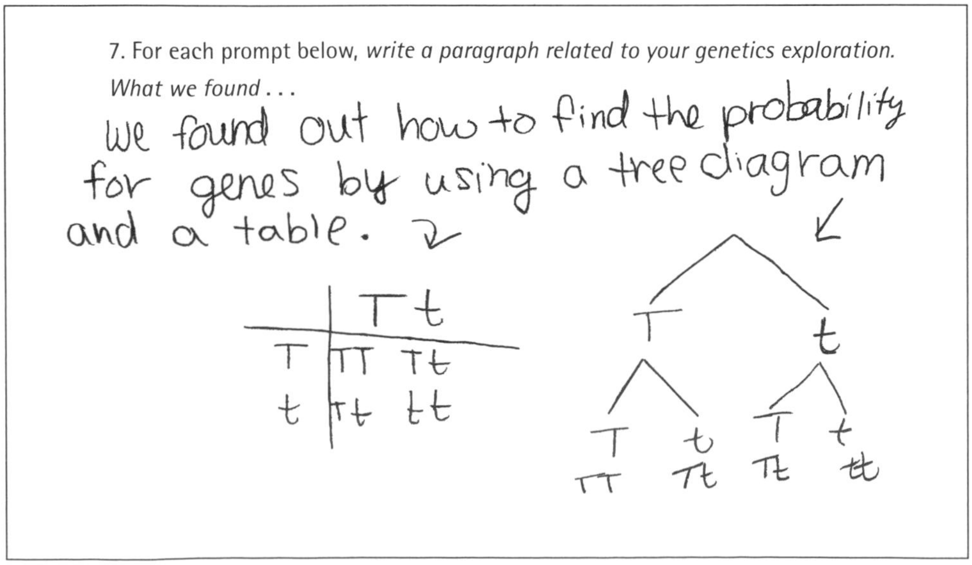

7. For each prompt below, *write a paragraph related to your genetics exploration.*

What we found . . .

We found out how to find the probability for genes by using a tree diagram and a table.

G Is for Googol
A Math Alphabet Book

G Is for Googol by David M. Schwartz (1998), is an encyclopedia of sorts, offering visuals and explanations of interesting mathematics from A to Z. For example, the letter S is for symmetry. The two-page discussion of symmetry includes examples of mirror symmetry, such as a comical face, a butterfly, a snowflake, and a circle. Rotational symmetry is also introduced, first with a pinwheel and then with a hubcap.

In this lesson, which focuses on geometry and measurement concepts, students create origami wreaths and pinwheels. Once students create these shapes, they analyze each to find both line and rotational symmetry. Students are asked to consider not just the shape, but the design on the shape (created with different colors). As an additional challenge, students dismantle their projects and analyze the folds made in the paper, identifying the types of triangles formed by the folding.

MATERIALS

5 paper polygons (see Blackline Masters) and scalene triangles

instructions for wreath and pinwheel origami, 1 copy per small group of students (see Blackline Masters)

6-by-6-inch origami paper in two different colors, 4 sheets of each color per student

angle rulers or protractors, 1 per student

G Is for Googol; s is for symmetry record sheets, 1 per student (see Blackline Masters)

pencils in 5 different colors, 1 of each color per student

optional: connecting rods

optional: uncooked spaghetti, about 50 pieces

Introducing the Investigation

I began by reading the title of the book to the class, *G Is for Googol*, and explained that this book had a math concept for every letter of the alphabet. I then read aloud "S Is for Symmetry," on pages 39–40. I explained that today, we would be making pinwheels out of origami paper and looking at symmetry. We would also unfold our papers and look at the shapes formed by the creases.

To make sure students had the appropriate vocabulary and concepts they needed for this lesson, I began with a warm-up that included looking at paper polygons and describing them in terms of their angles, sides, and symmetry.

I selected a triangle and asked, "What is this?"

Alyssa said, "An acute equilateral."

I asked, "What makes it acute?"

Patrick replied, "All the angles are less than ninety degrees."

"Does this triangle have any line or rotational symmetry?" I continued.

Courtney said, "It has a line down the middle."

"What do you mean, 'down the middle'?" I probed.

She clarified, "It goes from the top vertex to the middle of the side on the bottom."

I held a piece of uncooked spaghetti up to the triangle so the class could see the line of symmetry and asked, "Anything else?"

Kathryn asked, "Can't you do the line from all of the points?"

Marlo jumped in, "Yes, if you just turn the triangle, it is the same, so all three points can have a line of symmetry going to the middle of the side across from it."

"So there are three lines of symmetry?" I asked. "Any more?"

"It can rotate sixty degrees," Christopher added.

"What do the rest of you think about that?" I asked.

Timothy wasn't clear on this and asked, "If it rotates sixty degrees, it wouldn't be all the way to the next point yet, would it?"

Alyssa, building on this point, added, "Well if you rotate it [by sixty degrees] three times, it would only add up to a hundred and eighty degrees, so that is not enough."

I asked, "So, if you can rotate the triangle three times before it comes full circle, then can one of the rotations be sixty degrees? This is a tough one. Talk to your partner and use your angle rulers to explore."

After a brief pair share, students reported that the equilateral triangle had 120-degree rotational symmetry, meaning that when the triangle was rotated 120 degrees around its center, its points lined up with the positions of the points on the original shape.

I selected other triangles, such as an obtuse scalene and a right scalene. In a similar fashion, I asked students to describe the labels of each triangle and why those labels fit, then asked about the symmetry of the shapes. Students recognized that the scalene triangle did not have symmetry, the isosceles always had one line of symmetry, and the equilateral had three lines of symmetry. Finally, I selected a regular hexagon and we discussed its rotational symmetry of 60 degrees and its six lines of symmetry.

My students had some familiarity with origami because in previous lessons, we had spent some time on paper folding, constructing designs as a class and discussing mathematical concepts. With each new fold, I asked, "What do you see?" and students shared their observations. Students shared the following concepts and vocabulary during our discussions:

45-45-90 triangle	obtuse angle	right trapezoid
acute angle	parallel lines	right triangle
adjacent	parallelogram	rotation
alternate interior angles	pentagon	rotational symmetry
center	perimeter	segment
congruent	perpendicular lines	similar triangles
consecutive	plane	slope
diagonal	point	square
equidistant	polygon	transversal
hypotenuse	Pythagorean theorem	trapezoid
intersecting lines	quadrilateral	vertex
isosceles	rectangle	vertical angles
legs	rhombus	
lines of symmetry	right angle	

This process of modeling each fold and discussing the new shapes formed with each fold can be used for folding the papers for the wreath and pinwheels, especially if students have limited experience in folding papers or would benefit from the review of geometric shapes and properties. In this class, I let students work together to create the designs.

Observing the Students

Students worked in groups of four. As they moved to their groups, I gave each group a copy of the instructions for making the wreath and the pinwheel and handed each student eight squares of origami paper, four in one color and four in another color. I also directed them to have one group member get any additional tools they needed, like a piece of spaghetti, an angle ruler, or extra paper.

The wreath, which transforms into a pinwheel, takes eight pieces of origami paper. As they worked in their groups, students discussed the process of paper folding. This was a good opportunity for them to practice both reading instructions carefully and explaining precisely to their peers how to do a particular fold. When the wreath was completed, students carefully slid the sides to form the pinwheel. The shape could move back and forth between the wreath and the pinwheel. When students finished their construction, I handed out the *G Is for Googol; S Is for Symmetry* record sheets and instructed students to use their origami constructions to answer the questions.

As students worked on their sheets, I listened to the small-group discussions and debates that were occurring. Mariah, Devin, Matt, and Jessica were discussing how to determine line symmetry for the wreath. Mariah said, "It does have line symmetry because if you fold it, the sides match up."

Devin disagreed. He explained, "Look, if you fold it, the design is different. So if the color pattern is not the same, it isn't really symmetrical."

Looking at her record sheet, Jessica said, "Let's write that there is line symmetry for the shape only."

Jessica then reasoned, "If there are two possibilities for line symmetry, we should see if there are different answers for rotational symmetry."

Matt took the wreath and turned it, saying, "The first time it matches up, the colors don't match up, but the shape does."

"Let's draw two pictures," suggested Mariah, "one that is colored and one that is plain." (See Figure 7–1.)

As the students worked, they figured out that for every 45 degrees, the shape matched up, and for every 90 degrees, the colors also matched up. Therefore, there was rotational symmetry for the design at 90, 180, 270, and 360 degrees, and additional rotational symmetry for the shape at 45, 135, 225, and 315 degrees. This was true for both the wreath and the pinwheel.

Figure 7–1: This group showed rotational symmetry for both the design and the shape.

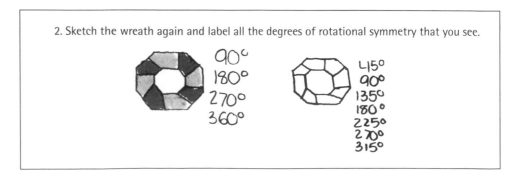

2. Sketch the wreath again and label all the degrees of rotational symmetry that you see.

Math and Nonfiction, Grades 6-8

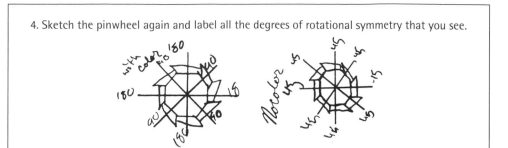

4. Sketch the pinwheel again and label all the degrees of rotational symmetry that you see.

Several groups were having trouble determining the degrees of rotation that produced rotational symmetry. Some students were taking the shortcut of dividing the number of sides into 360, but they couldn't see how the shape rotated physically. I asked the students to pause for a moment and suggested that they draw the angles of rotation from the center of the design. I also reminded students that they could use the spaghetti to help see the sections of the design that repeated. This was helpful to a number of students who used this strategy to measure the angles. (See Figure 7–2.)

A Class Discussion

Because rotational symmetry was challenging for students, I began the class discussion by asking, "How did you figure out what rotational symmetry the wreath and the pinwheel had?"

Kathryn explained, "I knew its total was three hundred sixty degrees, and then there are eight sides, so three hundred sixty divided by eight is forty-five, so it has forty-five-degree rotational symmetry. So, then I just kept adding on forty-five degrees, and we got forty-five degrees, ninety degrees, one hundred thirty-five degrees, one hundred eighty degrees, two hundred twenty-five degrees, two hundred seventy degrees, three hundred fifteen degrees, and three hundred sixty degrees."

"Does that always work?" I asked the class.

"No," Marti said with certainty. "It only works if the sides are all equal."

"The sides have to be equal to be symmetrical," Patrick restated.

Devin added, "Then the angles have to all be the same, too."

"The color matters, too," Mandy added. "So, you have to see if the colors match up."

I returned to the focus on strategies and asked, "What other ways did you use to figure the rotational symmetry?"

"We used our angle ruler," Timothy offered.

"Explain how you used your angle ruler," I encouraged.

"We placed it in the middle and then we measured the angle from one vertex to the other vertex. It came to forty-five degrees," Timothy elaborated.

I asked the class, "What do you think Timothy's group did after they had that first measurement to get the other measurements?"

"They can just put it in the calculator and keep adding forty-five degrees, like we did," Theresa offered.

"They could just keep using the angle measure and spread it out to the next point," Alyssa suggested.

"Timothy, what did your group do?" I asked.

"We measured the next one and then we saw that we could just add, so we did the rest by just adding until we got to three hundred sixty," he responded.

"What about line symmetry?" I asked.

"The pinwheel has no line symmetry, but the wreath does if you ignore the colors." Rachel said excitedly.

Patrick added, "If it was a perfect octagon wreath, it would have line symmetry, if you looked just at the shape, not at the design."

"If we had perfect octagons—let's just say our paper folding were perfect—what lines of symmetry would we have?" I asked.

I placed a wreath on the overhead and asked students to place a piece of spaghetti on the wreath where each line of symmetry would be. Some students had found only the four going from midpoint of one side to midpoint of another (maybe because of how they had positioned their drawing).

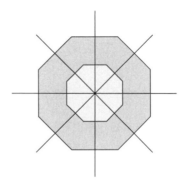

Mariah, representing her group, came up and laid four pieces of spaghetti, indicating the four lines of symmetry that went from one vertex to the opposite vertex.

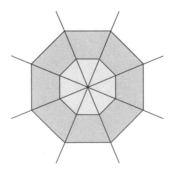

Several hands went up. I asked Mariah, "How did you know those were lines of symmetry?"

"Because if you fold on those lines, the sides match up."

"I see more hands. Are there more lines of symmetry?" I asked the class.

Patrick approached the overhead and showed four more lines, each one going from one vertex to the opposite vertex.

A Follow-Up Activity

I explained that after the students unfolded the wreath, their square pieces of paper would have many creases in them. Their task, I explained, was to find all the different types of triangles created by the folds in one piece of paper and then draw the triangles on their record sheet. I gave students pencils of different colors so they could more easily see the different triangles after recording them. (See Figures 7–3 and 7–4.)

After extensively exploring all the different-size triangles, students were surprised to see that every one was an isosceles right triangle (45°-45°-90°).

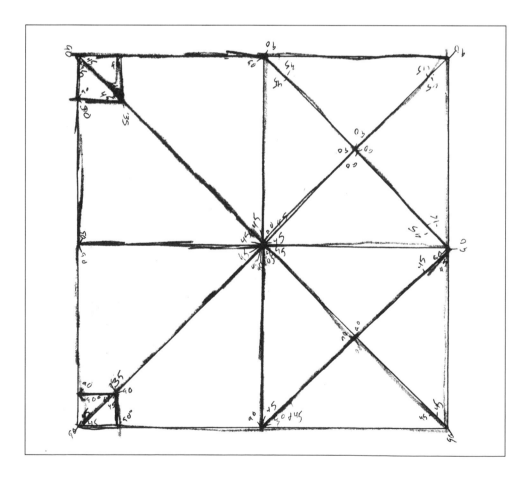

Figure 7–3: This student clearly outlined and labeled the different triangles he found.

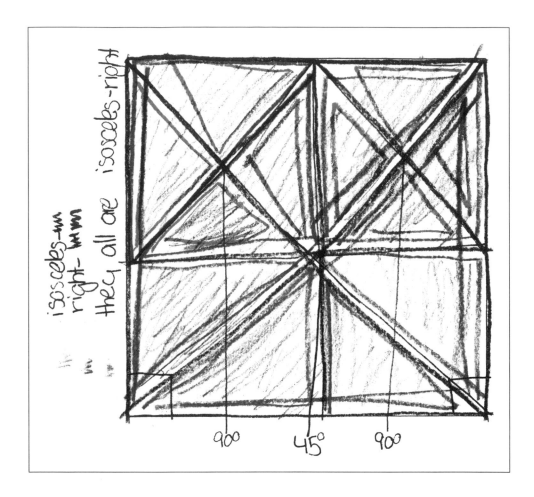

I asked students why they thought this might be true.

Patrick suggested it might be because they were always folding the paper in half at right angles, and half of ninety was forty-five. Devin added that they made a lot of diagonals that cut the square in half. We talked about all the diagonals splitting the square in half. Several students noted that the diagonals all bisected the corners. I asked students if they thought that all origami folding would create only isosceles right triangles. There was some discussion about whether this might be true or not and we left that thought to be explored on another day.

Students loved this activity because they liked moving the shape between the wreath and the pinwheel and because they could move the origami shape around to test for symmetry. It was also a good activity because they had to consider both the shape and the design, and the two forms created some interesting discussions about line and rotational symmetry.

If You Hopped Like a Frog

David M. Schwartz's picture book *If You Hopped Like a Frog* (1999) provides the reader with many opportunities to consider the proportional relationships between the human body and its abilities and various animal bodies and their abilities. For example, the opening pages explain that if you hopped like a frog, you could get to first base from home plate in just one leap. Using the different comparisons the author gives, students can work with weight, length, strength, and volume concepts.

This investigation focuses on proportional reasoning. Students use data about animals to determine what they would be able to do if they had abilities of those animals. Students explore five of the twelve comparisons presented in the book. As students work on their comparisons, they use a range of strategies to find equivalent ratios.

MATERIALS

calculators, 1 per student

If You Hopped Like a Frog task lists, 1 per student (see Blackline Masters)

optional: computer with Internet access or a set of encyclopedias

Introducing the Investigation

I began the lesson by reading *If You Hopped Like a Frog* to the students. I did not spend time on a discussion of the book at this point because I knew that it would follow the investigation. The students were very attentive. When I finished reading the book, I went back to the front and read the letter to the reader written by David Schwartz. I used the letter to launch the investigation.

I asked, "After hearing the story and the letter from David Schwartz, what would you say was his purpose for writing this book? I know that you talk about author's purpose in language arts class and I'm interested in how it applies here."

"I think he is trying to inform us and get us to think about how we relate to other animals," replied Bailey.

"Yeah, he is trying to teach us something," Will continued.

"I think he is trying to entertain us with the book—after all, it is a picture book," suggested David.

"Yes, but even kids' books have lessons in them. Think about fables and fairy tales. They are entertaining but usually have a moral," Bailey said.

"I think it is both, too," Ann said. "Lots of picture books are nonfiction and teach kids things about airplanes or living things or whatever. This book is like that, but it is written in a more entertaining way."

"Yeah, but I think he wrote the letter in the introduction to persuade us to use math!" John exclaimed.

"OK," I said, "sounds like we have some ideas about why David Schwartz wrote the book. Today we are going to answer the invitation to become engaged with the ideas in the book. We are going to make it more personal to us."

To begin the investigation, I divided students into groups and gave each student a calculator and a list of tasks. I explained that they were going to explore the animal facts that the author used in this book to determine what a human could do if he had the abilities of certain animals (data can be provided to students from the back of the book or students can research it on the Web or in an encyclopedia). I told them that they would be expected to share their results with the class along with their calculations and strategies.

I instructed the groups to read through all the tasks and start with the one that interested them the most. I also told them to complete the tasks in any order. I knew that not all groups would solve the tasks in the same way in the same amount of time. I hoped that each group would solve at least three of the tasks and that some groups would solve all five. This plan accommodated my diverse classroom. One group finished significantly faster than the other groups, so I gave it an extension, which was to brainstorm a list of other animals and their abilities.

A Class Discussion

Once all groups had finished at least three of the tasks, I had them stop and prepare for a class discussion.

"Who explored the crane's neck?" I asked.

"We did," Robert answered. "We found out that a crane's neck is one-third of his height. He is four feet with his neck, which is forty-eight inches. Since sixteen and forty-eight both divide by four, sixteen–forty-eighths simplifies to one-third. After that we took our height divided by three, which would give us the size of our neck if one of us was a crane. My neck would be twenty-one inches and Joseph's would be nineteen inches."

"Could we figure out how tall Robert and Joseph are if we knew what their necks would be like if they were a crane?" I asked.

"Yeah, we just have to multiply their neck by three because their neck is one-third of their body," Elizabeth responded.

"You wrote that you could use your long neck to look around things and that it would be hard to swallow—very true. However, you also wrote that you could see over heads and that you would bump your head on things. What's wrong with those statements?" I asked.

"You would still be the same height, just your neck would take up more of your body," answered Jill. "So if you couldn't see over people's heads before, then you wouldn't with your long neck either!"

"OK," I said. (See Figures 8–1 and 8–2.)

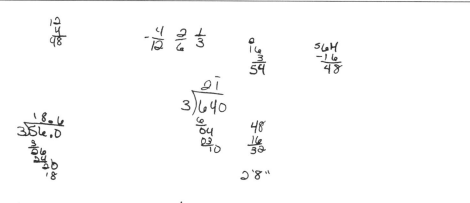

Figure 8–1: One student's work and explanation for the crane's neck task.

Figure 8–2: Another student's work and explanation for the crane's neck task.

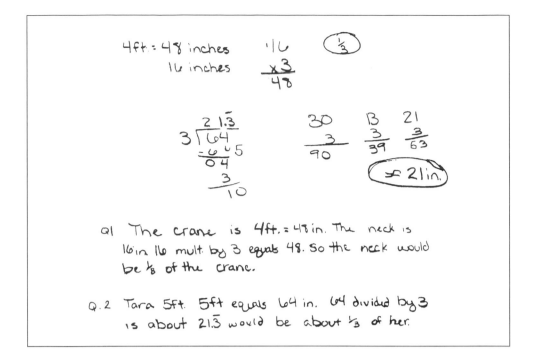

"Who looked into the ant task?" I asked.

"We did. We had a hard time at first because we couldn't agree on how to figure out how many times its body weight it could lift," Andrew said.

"What did you try?" I probed.

"Well, the ant weighs one–two hundred fiftieth of an ounce and it can lift one-fifth of an ounce. We noticed that two hundred fifty and five can divide by five. At first we kind of guessed that it could lift five times its body weight. When we checked and multiplied one–two hundred fiftieth by five, it didn't work because we got one-fiftieth, not one-fifth. To figure it out faster, we divided two hundred fifty by five and got fifty. We realized that we had to multiply by fifty, not five. That worked," Andrew explained.

"So what did you find you could lift?" I asked.

"Sam weighs about ninety pounds, so he could lift about four thousand, five hundred pounds. That's more than two tons. That's about how much a truck weighs," he answered. (See Figures 8–3 and 8–4.)

"Who did the pygmy shrew task?" I asked.

"We found out that a pygmy shrew eats about three times its body weight each day," Emily responded.

"How did you determine that?" I asked.

"We drew a picture at first. You see, it weighs one-fifth of an ounce, so we colored one-fifth of a circle. It eats three-fifths of an ounce, so we made another circle and colored in three-fifths of it. You can see that there are three one-fifths in three-fifths, so that's how we knew it would eat three times its body weight," Emily explained.

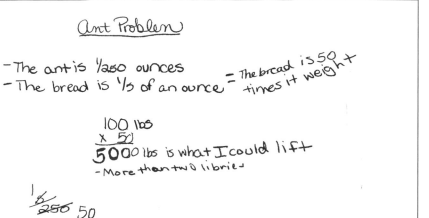

Figure 8–3: This student determined he could lift two small cars if he could lift like an ant.

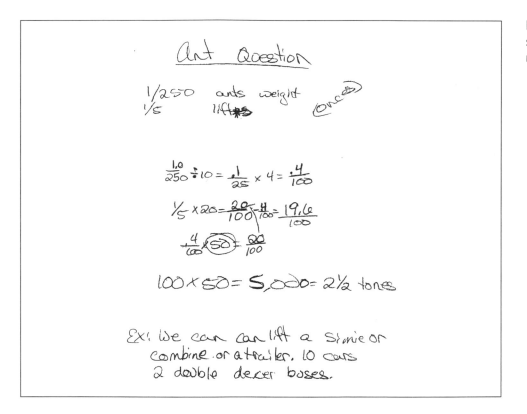

Figure 8–4: Another student's work and explanation for the ant task.

"Then what?" I probed.

"Well, then it got kind of hard because we weren't sure what to do about the quarter-pounders. We ignored that for a while and tried to figure out how much we would eat if we ate three times our body weight. We took an eighty-three-pound person, for example, and multiplied it by three to get two hundred and forty-nine pounds of food a day! That's a lot, but that's what it is like if you are a pygmy shrew!" she exclaimed.

"What about the quarter-pounders?" I probed.

"Yeah, well we finally figured out that four quarter-pounders would make a pound. You know, like four quarters make a dollar. So at first we wanted to divide by four, but that didn't make sense because we should have more quarter-pounders than the weight. Then we decided to multiply. We got nine hundred and ninety-six quarter-pounders. That still sounds like a lot!" Emily finished. (See Figures 8–5 and 8–6.)

"All right then. Donald, your group did those last two tasks and the frog task. Why don't you share what your group discovered about the frog?" I asked.

"We figured that the frog could jump twenty times his body. Then we figured that someone four feet ten inches could jump about ninety-six feet and eight inches," answered Donald.

"How did you figure that?" I questioned.

"We measured John and he was four feet ten inches. That makes him fifty-eight inches. Then we figured out that fifty-eight multiplied by twenty is one thousand, one hundred sixty inches. You said that it was hard to imagine all those inches, so we changed it into feet," he explained.

"How did you do that?" I asked.

"Just divided by twelve and we had eight left over," he continued.

"How did you know that the frog could jump twenty times its body length?" I asked.

Figure 8–5: The boys in this group determined they would each eat more than a thousand hamburgers a day if they ate like a pygmy shrew.

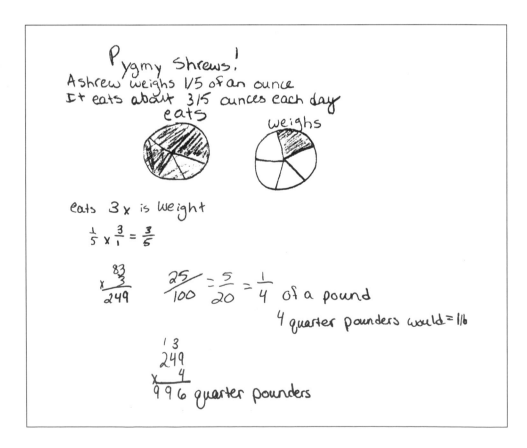

Math and Nonfiction, Grades 6-8

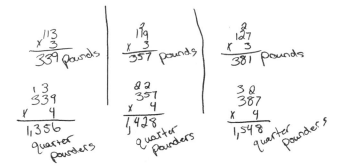

OK a pound is 16 oz and a quarter of it is 4 oz So we would have to eat 4 Mcdonalds quarter pounders. So they eat 3 times thier body wieght.

×113
× 3
339 pounds

×119
× 3
357 pounds

×127
× 3
381 pounds

339
× 4
1,356
quarter pounders

357
× 4
1,428
quarter pounders

387
× 4
1,548
quarter pounders

The steps we took were we found out 16 oz were one pound so we made it into 4s and that is 3 times his wieght so then we took our body wieght and multiplied it by 3 then we wanted to find out how many quarter pounders that we would have to eat so we found it took 4 to get a pound So we multiplied our wieght by 4 and got what we wanted. Our answer.

"At first we didn't get it, but you helped us when you asked us if sixty inches would be very far for us to jump. We figured not really because that is about how tall most of us are. Then we realized that if we could jump our height and the frog could jump our height, that would be really good for the frog because he is little compared to us. That's when we figured out that we needed to find how many frog heights were in sixty inches," he explained.

"What did you do?"

"We divided sixty by three and got twenty," he answered.

Other students shared their solutions to the frog task as well. For example, Lisa wrote:

We thought that a frog could jump 20 times its height because we took 60 divided by 3. An average human is about 5 feet 5 inches and that is 65 inches. Then we took 65 times 20 and got 1,300 inches. Then you would be able to jump 1,300 inches if you could jump like a frog.

See also another student's work in Figure 8–7.

A 3-inch frog can jump 60 inches. If I could jump like that I would jump about 1160 inches being 58 inches tall.

Which would equal 96 ft 8 in.

$$12\overline{)1160}$$ = 960 ... 108, 0080, 72, 8

An example is 12 8 ft tall room stacked up on top of each other and laid down on the ground would be 12 rooms and 1 in.

$$8\overline{)96}$$ = 12 ... 8, 16, 16, 0

"Well, last question, last group, what about the brachiosaurus problem?" I asked.

"We didn't like this problem very much," Steven replied.

"Oh, why not?" I asked.

"The numbers were so big and also so small. We also didn't like that it was in kilograms. We had to change it to pounds and we didn't know how," he explained.

"Did you learn something that you could tell us about, though?" I asked.

"I guess, but it was hard," Steven answered.

"Tell us what you did," I said, trying to encourage him.

"First we changed eighty thousand to grams and got eighty million grams because there are a thousand grams in one kilogram. Then we divided eighty million by two hundred [the weight of the brain] and got four hundred thousand. So the brain of the brachiosaurus is four hundred thousand times smaller than its body," Steven explained.

"What fraction of the body weight is that?" I asked.

"It is one–four hundred thousandth," Carol answered.

"So what did you find out about the human brain?" I asked.

"Well, if Chase weighs ninety-five pounds then we took ninety-five divided by four hundred thousand and got 2.375 E −4. We didn't know what that means so we had to ask," explained Steven.

"Who can explain what that means?" I probed.

"We found out 2.345 E −4 is in scientific notation. It's 2.375 times ten to the power of negative four. You have to move the decimal four places to the left so 0.0002375 is what we got. That's so small! We found out an ounce would be one sixteenth or 0.0625 as a decimal so it's still much lighter than that. We figured it would be like a grain of sand!" exclaimed Carol.

To conclude the lesson, I had the group with extra time share the list that it had brainstormed. Other students added a few suggestions. This lesson enabled students to further develop and strengthen their concepts of ratio and enhance their number sense. In addition, students typed up their solutions to make their own class book.

The Motley Fool Investment Guide for Teens

Eight Steps to Having More Money Than Your Parents Ever Dreamed Of

The Motley Fool Investment Guide for Teens, by David and Tom Gardner (2002), provides eight steps to having more money. The authors introduce Step 1, set goals (and reach them), by asking readers what *rich* means. In a culturally sensitive way, the authors address the extremes in the world, from earning two dollars a day to owning mansions in three different countries. They make the point that it is reasonable to want to own a house you love and be able to do things that give you pleasure. The financial focus of the book is important to young teens, who need opportunities to think about their future dreams and how to realize them.

In this investigation, students explore linear and exponential growth situations. They use the patterns they find in these growth situations to write an algebraic rule for finding the amount of money they would have after investing a certain amount for any number of years. Students investigate various growth rate percents and the time it takes to double one's money. This leads to the "rule of seventy-two."

MATERIALS

calculators, 1 per student

The Motley Fool Investment Guide for Teens **record sheets,** 1 per student (see Blackline Masters)

Introducing the Investigation

I began by reading the title and subtitle of the book to the class. Then I read the section about Anne Scheiber, on pages 13–15.

I told the students to imagine that they had one hundred dollars to invest at a growth rate of 10 percent per year. Next I asked, "What is ten percent of one hundred?"

Suzy answered, "Ten percent means ten out of one hundred, so they would earn ten dollars interest on their money the first year."

"So how much would you have at the end of the first year?" I asked.

"You add the ten dollars to the one hundred dollars because it is money that you earned, so now you have one hundred and ten dollars," Keagan stated.

"What about the next year?" I continued.

"Would you just add ten dollars again?" asked Sean.

"No, you would have to do it all over again. Find ten percent of one hundred ten dollars and then add that to the one hundred ten dollars," Janice replied.

"Why?" Sean asked.

"Because you earn ten percent on the money you have. If you have more money, you will earn more interest. Think about it this way— would you rather have ten percent of one hundred dollars or ten percent of two hundred dollars?" Janice asked.

"I'd rather have ten percent of two hundred dollars," Sean answered.

"Exactly. When you add the interest on, your money grows each year, which means you earn more money the next year and so on!" Janice exclaimed.

"It seems that you noticed that we continue with the same procedure over and over again," I said. "Is there another way to include your one hundred and ten dollars other than adding it back on every time? Is there a way to combine the two steps to make one step?"

After a long silence, a student meekly answered, "I don't think so."

"Let's think through this a little more carefully," I responded. "First, how do you find ten percent of one hundred dollars?" I asked.

Larry chimed right in, saying, "Well, I just multiply ten-hundredths times one hundred. That's how I got ten on the first try."

"OK, did anyone else multiply ten-hundredths by one hundred?" I asked. The majority of the hands went up in the air. "Then let's continue with this multiply idea you have going here. What could you multiply one hundred by to get your money back? In other words, what do you multiply one hundred by to get one hundred?"

Sue answered quickly, "That's easy—one, because one hundred times one is one hundred."

"Instead of multiplying one hundred by ten-hundredths to get the interest and then multiplying one hundred by one to get your money back, and adding them together in the end, is there any way to combine these steps?" I asked.

"Oh I get it," John said with some excitement. "If you add the one and ten-hundredths together first, you can multiply one hundred by one hundred and ten percent or one and one tenths and get one hundred and ten dollars in one step!"

"Let's try another one," I said. "What if you had one hundred dollars and you grew it by five percent a year for ten years? Discuss with your partner two ways you could find how much money you would have in ten years."

As I walked around, students discussed how to change 5 percent to a decimal and how to find 5 percent of a hundred dollars. A popular technique was to use calculators to do it "the long way"—that is, students were multiplying the original amount of money by 0.05 and then adding the result to the original amount. The original amount of money changed each year, so for each calculation, they were entering the original amount and the percentage and then adding them to get the new original amount. One group was having a discussion about how to get the increased (new) amount from the original in one step. They decided to multiply the original value by 1.05, which they reported later as "the short way." As Lauren explained to the class, "Multiplying by one gives you your money back and multiplying by five-hundredths gives you your little bit of interest, so you get a little more than what you had each time you do this." An advantage of this approach is that on the calculator, it involves a single step of multiplying what is on the screen (the existing year's amount) by 1.05 to get the new amount for the new year.

A Class Discussion

Next, I handed out the record sheets and asked students to fill in the first table, working until their money doubled from the original amount. In the case of 5 percent compound interest, this would take approximately fifteen years. Next I read the section titled "The Growth Rate" in the middle of page 18 in *The Motley Fool Investment Guide for Teens*. I asked the students to fill in the remaining two tables on their record sheet until their money doubled for 11 percent and 13 percent interest. After students completed the tables, I asked them to share what they noticed. (See Figure 9–1.)

"The table for thirteen percent has bigger numbers and doubles sooner," John answered.

"Obviously the table for five percent has smaller numbers and takes longer to double," replied Peyton.

"Would it surprise you if I told you there was a shorter way to find out when your money would double?" I asked with a smile. "I learned from reading this book about something called the rule of seventy-two."

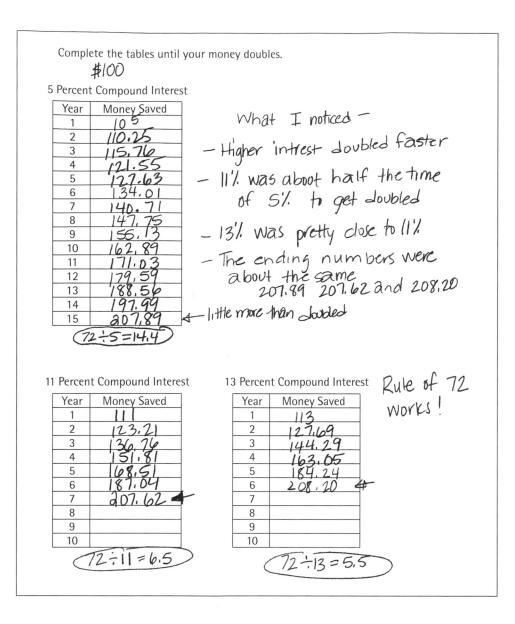

Complete the tables until your money doubles.

$100

5 Percent Compound Interest

Year	Money Saved
1	105
2	110.25
3	115.76
4	121.55
5	127.63
6	134.01
7	140.71
8	147.75
9	155.13
10	162.89
11	171.03
12	179.59
13	188.56
14	197.99
15	207.89

72 ÷ 5 = 14.4

← little more than doubled

What I noticed —

— Higher intrest doubled faster

— 11% was aboot half the time of 5% to get doubled

— 13% was pretty close to 11%

— The ending numbers were about the same
207.89 207.62 and 208.20

11 Percent Compound Interest

Year	Money Saved
1	111
2	123.21
3	136.76
4	151.81
5	168.51
6	187.04
7	207.62
8	
9	
10	

72 ÷ 11 = 6.5

13 Percent Compound Interest

Year	Money Saved
1	113
2	127.69
3	144.29
4	163.05
5	184.24
6	208.20
7	
8	
9	
10	

72 ÷ 13 = 5.5

Rule of 72 works!

Figure 9–1: One student's completed record sheet.

At this point I read "The Rule of 72" from inside the box on page 21. The rule of seventy-two is a technique for figuring when your money will double. The formula is simple: just divide 72 by the growth rate. For example, if the interest rate is 8 percent, then the money will double in nine years because 72 ÷ 8 = 9.

After reading, I said, "Try this calculation using five percent, ten percent, thirteen percent, fifteen percent, and twenty percent."

Students worked on their calculations. When they were finished, I asked, "Do you notice any relationships among these numbers?"

"I think that the number of years until it doubles at ten percent is half the number of years until it doubles at five percent," Morgan remarked.

Curtis added, "Yeah, and the number of years until it doubles at twenty percent is half the number of years until it doubles at ten percent."

"I see another one!" exclaimed Tia. "It takes three times longer to double with five percent compared to fifteen percent!"

The students continued with this discussion, finding patterns with 5 percent and 20 percent too.

Then I asked them to find when their money would double if they earned 50 percent interest per year. When they calculated it using the rule of seventy-two, they got 1.44. We discussed what this meant and they determined that it was almost a year and a half. To really get them thinking, I asked them to find when their money would double if they got very lucky and earned 75 percent interest per year. When they calculated it using the rule of seventy-two, they got 0.96. We discussed what this meant. Their answer was less than 1 because it would take less than one year to double their money at 75 percent! The next question logically followed: "What percent interest would you have to earn in a year to double your money in exactly one year?" The answer, of course, is 72 percent because 72 ÷ 72 = 1!

A Follow-Up Task

To help students get a better visual of this type of growth rate, I had them graph the money they would earn with 10 percent interest over

Figure 9–2: Graph showing growth of $100 earning 10 percent interest each year for twenty years.

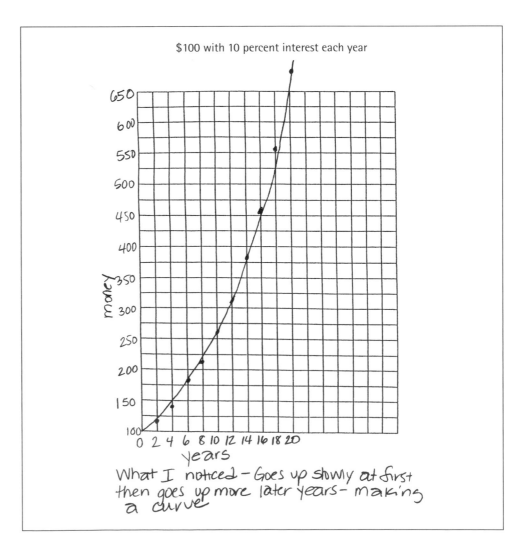

Math and Nonfiction, Grades 6–8

twenty years in two-year intervals. (See Figure 9–2.) I then had them make another table showing how much they'd make if they started with $100 and earned exactly $20 in interest each year for twenty years. Finally, I had them make a graph of this data. (See Figure 9–3.)

I asked them how the graphs compared.

"This one, the ten percent graph, kind of curves upward but the other one, the twenty-dollar graph, goes up in a straight line," Curtis answered.

"The one with the straight line is going up faster for a little while, but then the curve takes a turn and passes it up," continued Will.

"They both start at the same place," Bailey added.

"Why do they start at the same place on the graph?" I asked.

"Because we started both these plans with the same amount of money—one hundred dollars. So when we graphed them we started out with the same amount at zero years," Bailey answered.

"Great!" I responded. "What we've studied today are linear and exponential models. Can you tell me which is which?"

The students correctly identified the graphs and we ended the discussion with a brief summary.

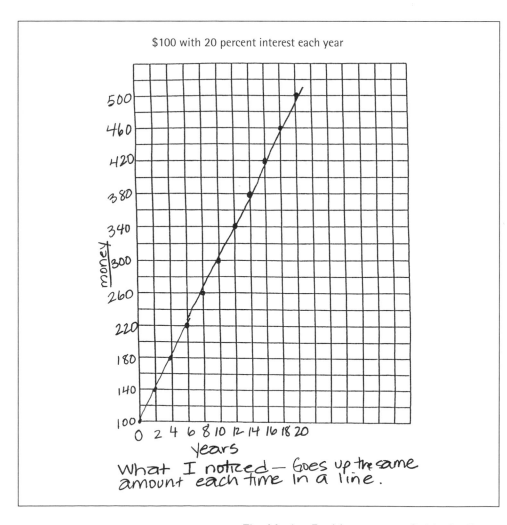

Figure 9–3: Graph showing growth of $100 earning $20 interest each year for twenty years.

A Negro League Scrapbook

A Negro League Scrapbook, a picture book by Carole Boston Weatherford (2005), contains interesting facts about many of the great players of the Negro Baseball League. Buck O'Neil, a former Negro League player and lifelong advocate for education and opportunities for all, wrote the foreword. The many photos capture the essence of the times and the country's enthusiasm for baseball.

Satchel Paige is one of the great pitchers in baseball history. Pictures and facts about him and other pitchers are provided, including how many shutouts, no-hitters, and wins Paige had. No one in Major League Baseball has come close to matching his statistics.

In this investigation, students make mathematical comparisons to show how incredible Satchel Paige really was. They analyze data and write a sports column using their findings. The mathematics of this lesson involves computation, fractions, percents, percent of increase, number sense, and estimation.

MATERIALS

calculators, 1 per student

A Negro League Scrapbook record sheets,
  1 per student (see Blackline Masters)

Introducing the Investigation

I began this lesson by holding up the picture book *A Negro League Scrapbook* and asking if anyone had heard about the league and could share anything about it. Several students said, "Jackie Robinson."

"Yes," I said, "Jackie Robinson was in the Negro League. Can you think of anyone else?" I happened to be lucky enough to have a baseball signed by Buck O'Neil, and I tossed it out to the class. I asked the student who caught it to read the name on the baseball. I then opened the book and read the foreword that had been written by him. Both the foreword and the signature on my baseball were written shortly before he died at age ninety-two. In the foreword, O'Neil points out that the Negro League was not just a sports league but an important part of history, offering black men a chance at an education.

I then read various passages from the book, sharing some statistics about the greats in the league. In particular, I focused on the pages about Satchel Paige. When I finished reading about Paige, I asked if the students knew any other great pitchers. Suggestions included Cy Young and Nolan Ryan.

I explained to students that today they were going to be using mathematical statements to describe and compare baseball statistics. I distributed calculators and the *Negro League Scrapbook* record sheets. I asked students to study the table and see what information jumped out at them.

"Satchel Paige has four times as many wins as Cy Young, who has the most in the Major Leagues," Paul said.

"I like that statement because it has a mathematical comparison," I said. "Who can tell me what the comparison was?"

"That Satchel has four times more," offered Lisa.

"Great," I said. "I want you to have time to think of some of your own ways to compare and explain how unique Satchel Paige was, so we will save the rest of our comparisons for later in the lesson."

I asked students to work on the activity in their small groups of two to three students, but to record on their own individual sheets.

Observing the Students

The students were very skilled at finding percents, so they worked fairly quietly and quickly, adding up the totals from the table and determining what percent of wins Satchel Paige had among these greats (58 percent). (See Figure 10–1.) We recently had discussed percent increase, so in one group the students decided to explore the percent increase of Satchel Paige over the others. (See Figure 10–2.)

The next item on the handout presented the open-ended challenge of using mathematics to create comparisons. As I saw students moving on to this question, I asked them to pause.

"Remember, as you think of comparisons, you want to find ways to illustrate how great Satchel was *and* be creative, thinking of comparisons that other groups might not think of."

Figure 10–1: This student
clearly recorded the calculations she did to compare
Satchel Paige to the group
of greats.

1. The table below shows information about five great pitchers. What percent
of wins among these greats did Satchel Paige have? What percent of shutouts
among these five did he have? What percent of no-hitters?

	Wins	Shutouts	No-Hitters	Different Kinds of Pitches
Roger Clemens	348	46	0	5
Nolan Ryan	324	61	7	5
Greg Maddox	335	35	0	5
Cy Young	511	76	3	6
Satchel Paige	2,100	300	55	14

Wins 348+324+335+511+2100 = 3618 Satchels total wins
$\frac{2100}{3618}$ =58%

Shutouts 46+61+35+76+300 = 518 Paige total shutouts 300/ $\frac{5804}{518}$ =58%
5791

No Hitters 0+7+0+3+55 = 65 Satchels total shutouts
55/65 =85%
84.61

Figure 10–2: One group decided to explore the percent
increase of Satchel Paige
over the others.

1. The table below shows information about five great pitchers. What percent
of wins among these greats did Satchel Paige have? What percent of shutouts
among these five did he have? What percent of no-hitters?

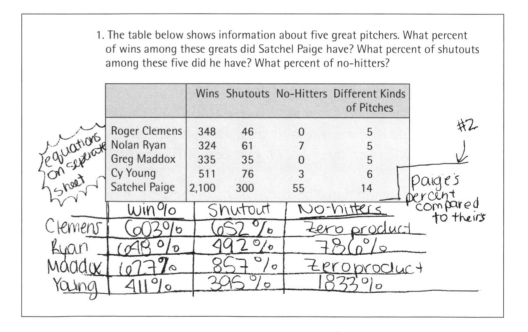

equations on separate sheet

#2

Paige's percent compared to theirs

	Win%	Shutout	No-hitters
Clemens	603%	652%	zero product
Ryan	648%	492%	786%
Maddox	677%	857%	zero product
Young	411%	395%	1833%

Marco, Sarah, and Libby were working on comparing the shutouts.
They began by averaging the Major League Baseball pitchers, getting
fifty-five shutouts. From here, they began to question their process.

Sarah said, "So we take three hundred divided by fifty-five to get
the percent for Satchel Paige."

They all computed this on the calculator and wrote down *5.45.*

"So, Satchel Paige had five point forty-five percent more . . . that
doesn't make sense," Libby remarked.

"Wait, it's fifty-four and a half; then Satchel Paige had fifty-four and a half percent more," Sarah stated.

Marco interjected, "No, you multiply by one hundred, so you get five-hundred forty-five."

"So it's five-hundred forty-five percent? No, I think we need to add a decimal point—five and forty-five–hundredths."

Libby reasoned, "So you multiply by one hundred and get five-hundred forty-five. I don't think you can have five-hundred forty-five percent."

I interjected because they had lost track of what they were looking for. "What would forty-five percent or five-hundred forty-five percent or five point forty-five percent represent?"

"How much more Satchel had than the average of the others," Libby stated.

"So you would have five-hundred forty-five percent more—that seems like a lot," Marco said, puzzled.

They were stuck. I said, "If Satchel Paige had one hundred percent of the shutouts that the others had (on average), how many would he have had?"

After some think time, Marco said, "Wouldn't one hundred percent mean he had all, so he would have fifty-five?"

"Do the two of you agree?" I asked. The girls nodded.

"So, if Satchel had two hundred percent of the shutouts, what would that mean?"

They all stated, "One hundred ten."

"Now, go back to your dilemma and see if you can use these steps to help you decide what your statement is," I requested.

I left the group and returned a little later, asking for someone to explain what the students had decided. Libby said, "We figured out that the five-hundred forty-five percent meant that was the percent more that Satchel had. That is something like having five times more, which is right, because he had five and forty-five–hundredths times more, so five hundred forty-five percent."

In another group, Leo, Andrew, and Randy were wondering if they could find some kind of algebraic relationship. They reasoned that if they took the pitchers in order of number of wins, the numbers increased in what looked like exponential growth. They began entering their data into the Stat Plot function of their calculator to see if they could run a linear regression and get an equation to describe the growth. As interesting as this notion was, I asked them what conditions would have to be true for them to be designing an equation.

"An independent and dependent variable," Leo said.

"What would they be in this case?" I asked.

"The independent is what player we put down and the dependent is the number of their wins," Randy replied.

"So, the line you drew to connect the points, what does it represent?" I asked.

"The trend in how it's growing," Leo replied.

"Then what happens between the points and what happens after Satchel Paige? Are you saying that the next player greater than Satchel would have to be much higher on your graph?" I asked, glad that they were stretching their thinking, but wanting to make sure they were clear that this wasn't a situation that was going to fit a mathematical model or equation.

"No, it doesn't work for that, but we like it because it shows that Satchel was exponentially better than the other pitchers," Leo said, smiling.

I couldn't argue with this and the group was having a great discussion of exponential functions, so I reminded the boys to make sure they came up with all the statements they needed and moved to another group.

Allison, Miranda, and Clayton were working on a statistical approach.

"Can we do a box-and-whisker plot?" Allison asked. "That would really show what an outlier Satchel Paige is."

"Well, we don't have enough data to call him an outlier . . . we need one more pitcher," Clayton stated. They stopped and raised their hands.

"Can we do a box-and-whisker plot?" they asked me.

"Why would you use a box-and-whisker plot?"

Allison explained, "We think it would show that Satchel Paige is an outlier."

"But we need another pitcher to do it," added Miranda.

"If you want to add another pitcher, it would be OK. You can look up someone on the Major League Baseball website. Be sure to find a pitcher that was inducted into the Hall of Fame; that way you can still say he was a great pitcher."

I left the group. In the end, these students decided not to do a box-and-whisker plot, but I made a mental note to use this book, in particular Satchel Paige's statistics, when teaching outliers with mean, median, and box-and-whisker plots. I would add a few more pitchers to the list.

A Class Discussion

After each group had written at least two comparison statements, we stopped to do some sharing. Students volunteered, came to the front of the room, and shared their statement, first reading it and then telling how they performed their calculations. There was a wide range in the number of statements made by the groups and in the level of mathematics used.

For example, Casie reported, "Satchel Paige has four times as many shutouts as any other pitcher. We figured this out by taking Satchel's shutouts and dividing them by the shutouts for each of the other players. The closest was Cy Young, but Satchel had more than four times that much."

Zachary said, "Mine is about the No-Hitters column. Satchel not only has more than all the others put together, he has forty-five more than all the others!"

"We said that Satchel has eighty-five percent of all the no-hitters," Samuel interjected.

Several other groups chimed in with what they had stated about the no-hitters.

Jasmine raised her hand. "I figured out that Satchel had three hundred of the five hundred eighteen shutouts of all the pitchers combined, which is about fifty-seven point ninety-two percent."

"I found out that Satchel had three hundred nineteen percent more wins than Cy," Aimee contributed. (See Figures 10–3 through 10–5 for more comparison statements.)

---

2. Satchel Paige's statistics are not listed on the Major League Baseball (MLB) website, except for the few years toward the end of his career when he was in the MLB. What comparisons do you notice between Satchel Paige's pitching statistics and those of other great pitchers? Make three to five mathematical comparisons and list them below:

1. In the Wins category he made up more half of the number of wins for all 5 of the pitcher's with 58%
2. In shutouts he also made up more then half of them with 57%
3. In no-hitters he made up more the 3/4 of them with 84% of the no-hitters.
4. In all 4 categories satchel leads with most wins, shutouts, no-hitters + the number of pitches
5. In all 4 categories he makes at leats half of the total number

Figure 10–3: This student used statements as a benchmark in comparison to Satchel Paige.

---

2. Satchel Paige's statistics are not listed on the Major League Baseball (MLB) website, except for the few years toward the end of his career when he was in the MLB. What comparisons do you notice between Satchel Paige's pitching statistics and those of other great pitchers? Make three to five mathematical comparisons and list them below:

① Satchel's wins are 400% greater than Cy Young's.
② Satchel has 8 more pitches than Cy Young.
③ Satchel had 254 more shutouts than Roger Clemens.
④ Satchel had 48 more no-hitters than Nolan Ryan.
⑤ Satchel had 1776 more wins than Nolan Ryan.

Figure 10–4: This student created statements comparing Satchel Paige to another pitcher.

Figure 10–5: This student
determined how many more
times Satchel Paige had
done each accomplishment.

2. Satchel has had 5.5 times as many no-hitters
than any of the other pitchers put together
7+3=10   55/10=5.5

b. Satchel had 582 more wins than all
of roger nolan, greg & cy
348 + 374 + 335 + 511 = 1518
2100 - 1518 = 582

C. Satchel had 36% more shutouts than
Roger, Nolan & Greg
46+61+35+300=442   300/442=.678 =68%
46+61+35=142   142/442=.321=32%   68% 32% = 36%

d. Satchel had quadruple as many wins as
Cy young 2100/511=4.1

e. Satchel had twice as many kind of pitches
as Cy young.
14/6 = 2.33

Because class was about to end, we decided to save the third task on the record sheet for the next day.

Day 2: Wrapping Up the Investigation

The next day, students arrived excited to get to work on their sports columns about Satchel (the last task 3 on the record sheet). They worked for about twenty minutes and then presented their stories to the class, taking about two minutes each. This provided an opportunity for students to share their unique findings and creative writing and to ask questions. Here's one of the class's favorite stories, written as a script:

Emily: *Hi! I'm Satchella Paige. As you may have guessed, I am Satchel Paige's long lost twin sister, eight times removed. Believe me, I know all of his wonderful statistics.*

Tremendous Negro baseball player, Satchel Paige, has an outstanding record and his statistics soar over Major League ball players. He has surpassed Cy Young's win record of 511 games by 300 percent. He has won 2,100 games! Roger Clemens, Nolan Ryan, and Greg Maddox all have five different pitches. Satchel Paige has fourteen. That's almost a 2 percent increase! Nolan Ryan's statistics show he has had shutouts in about sixty games; Paige has had three hundred. That is a 500 percent increase! But wait, there's more! Roger Clemens has never had a game where no hits were made. Satchel Paige has had fifty-five!

Now for the official Sports Talk Satchel Expert, we'll go to Alfreda Wintergreen. She will explain the math behind the stats of this magnificent ball player.

Stephanie: *Thanks, Satchella, now for some statistics updates. [Stephanie went on to share how they figured the percent increase.]*

See Figures 10–6 through 10–10 for more students' stories.

---

3. Sports writers like to showcase the skills of great players. Use a separate piece of paper to write a brief sports column about Satchel Paige and his incredible talent. Use percents in your column to compare the pitchers.

Have You Played with the best?

Have you played with the best? well Satchel paige is the best. I mean when you win 4X as many wins as Cy Young, that's amazing. So if you think you're the best try hitting off of Satchel Paige

Figure 10–6: This student's sports column captures how great Satchel Paige was.

The brilliant pitcher Satchel Paige has had an amazing season! He used his incredible skill to win 310% more games than the next best pitcher, Cy Young. He has also had 295% more shutouts, 1733% more no-hitters, and 133% more pitches! What a pitcher!

My Work

* Wins: Satchel - 2100, Cy - 511
increase - 2100 - 511 = 1589
increase/starting number - 1589/511 = 3.109589
or 310%

* Shutouts: satchel - 300, Cy - 76
increase - 300 - 76 = 224
increase/starting number - 224/76 = 2.9473684...

* no-hitters: satchel - 55, Cy - 3   or 295%
increase - 55 - 3 = 52
increase/starting number - 52/3 = 17.3 or 1733%

* pitches: satchel - 14, Cy - 6
increase - 14 - 6 = 8
increase/starting number - 8/6 = 1.3 or 133%

Figure 10–7: This student's sports column uses percents to emphasize the greatness of Satchel Paige.

Figure 10–8: This student's sports column includes fascinating facts along with comparisons.

You may have heard of Roger Clemens, Nolan Ryan, Greg Maddox, and Cy Young. How about Satchel Paige. He was a huge all-star in the Negro League. Most people are stunned when they hear his statistics. He has $\frac{300}{518}$ of the shutouts of all of these pitchers combined. With 2100 wins, Satchel Paige has more wins than all of the other great pitchers combined. He also had more than 84% of the no-hitters pitched by these all-time greats. Satchel Paige also had a towering 14 pitches. That is over 2 times more than any of the other pitches. His most famous being his fastball. His Major League stats are what people see, but his major accomplishments are those that came in the Negro League.

Figure 10–9: This student's sports column compares Satchel Paige to other great pitchers.

3. Sports writers like to showcase the skills of great players. Use a separate piece of paper to write a brief sports column about Satchel Paige and his incredible talent. Use percents in your column to compare the pitchers.

Satchel Paige was one of the world's greatest pitchers. For instance, Satchel's wins were 4x greater than Cy Young's. Paige also had 254 more shut outs than Roger Clemens. Compared to Greg Maddox who had no no-hitters Paige had 55. Now that was a genius of a pitcher

Always A Superstar

Satchel Paige was "always a superstar" in the 60s. He had an awesome number of wins, shutouts, no hitters, & different kinds of pitches. He had 58% of wins out of 4 other great pitchers. On a graph that was conducted, Satchel's # of wins was an outliar compared to the other 4 great pitchers. His average is also the greatest among all the individual averages. The 4 other great pitchers include: Roger Clemens, Nolan Ryan, Greg Maddox, and Cy Young. These pitchers have not met Satchel's high scores yet. The percent increases are interesting: from Nolan - Greg there is a 3% increase, from Greg - Roger there is a 4% increase, from Roger - Cy there is a 47% increase, from Cy - Satchel there is a 311% increase. This is Stefanie Jones reporting statistics for baseball!

Figure 10–10: This student's sports column reports comparisons among the great pitchers.

One Thousand Paper Cranes

The Story of Sadako and the Children's Peace Statue

The story of Sadako Sasaki became well known in America through *Sadako and the Thousand Paper Cranes* and *Sadako* by Eleanor Coerr. In *One Thousand Paper Cranes*, Takayuki Ishii (1997) writes a nonfiction version of the story. In 1955 Sadako died of leukemia, caused by exposure to radiation from the atomic bomb dropped in 1945 on Hiroshima. Sadako thought that if she could make one thousand cranes, her wish to stay alive would come true. Her story so touched the hearts of others that her image appears at the top of the Children's Peace Statue in Hiroshima Peace Memorial Park.

For this lesson, which focuses on geometry concepts, students create an asymmetrically shaped bird whose image they use to perform rigid transformations on a coordinate axis. Specifically, students use the *x*- and *y*-axes to reflect the nonsymmetrical image of their origami bird and draw conclusions about the relationship of the coordinates of the original shape to those of the reflected shape.

MATERIALS

protractor, 1 per student

6-by-6-inch origami paper, at least 2 sheets per student

transparency of grid paper with coordinate axes in center (see Blackline Masters)

grid paper with coordinate axes in center, 1 sheet per student

optional: graphing calculators (with Stat Plot function), 1 per student

optional: rulers, 1 per student

optional: how to make a (basic) origami bird instructions, 1 copy per student (see Blackline Masters)

Preparing for the Investigation

Prior to this lesson, students had used diagrams to do some simple paper folding. They had also made wreaths and pinwheels, which involved using multiple pieces of origami paper (see "G Is for Googol" on page 49). Students therefore knew how to do basic origami folds. If your students do not have experience with origami, I recommend selecting any basic origami construction as a beginning experience prior to doing this investigation. These can be found on a Web search or in the many available origami books, such as *The Joy of Origami* by Margaret van Sickle.

The day before this lesson, I asked my students to do the following assignment on rotational symmetry, using a protractor:

> *Using a circle, inscribe a hexagon by measuring angles. Once the hexagon is drawn, create a design on the template that will have 60-degree rotational symmetry.*

Introducing the Investigation

I began the lesson by asking students, "Who has a design that has sixty-degree rotational symmetry?" referring to the task they had completed the day before. As I held up each volunteer's design, I asked the other students if they agreed.

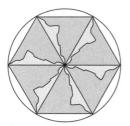

The design is the same
at a 60-degree rotation.

When students disagreed, I had them work in pairs to decide what kind of symmetry the design did have. Brea's design did not have 60-degree rotational symmetry, but did have 180-degree rotational symmetry.

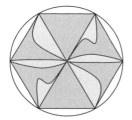

This design is repeated
at 180 degrees.

Next I held up the book *One Thousand Paper Cranes* and asked, "How many of you know the story of Sadako?" A few students shared what they knew. I then read aloud passages of the book about Sadako's creation of the cranes (pages 58–60) and the creation of the Children's Peace Statue (pages 74–81). The class listened intently.

I asked if any of the students had made origami birds before. Several had. I shared with the class the instructions for the crane we would be making. To date, they had folded paper to make figures that had symmetrical designs, but the crane has no symmetry and involves more complex paper folding.

The instructions for creating the crane are in the back of *One Thousand Paper Cranes* on page 95. I gave each student two sheets of origami paper, placed a transparency of the instructions on the overhead, and asked the students to create the crane. I also asked them to see how many different types of triangles and other polygons they noticed in the shape as they worked. Making the crane takes some time and is of medium difficulty, and it could be done as homework instead of in class. If students have not done origami before, you may opt to give them the instructions for making a basic origami bird in the Blackline Masters.

Once students had finished their birds, I asked, "What symmetry does the bird have?" Students noted the "aerial view" had line symmetry. I asked students to look at the side view of the crane (see illustration 9 of basic origami bird instructions on page 95) and see if its shadow had any symmetry. It is not symmetrical; therefore, it is a good shape for introducing transformations on a coordinate plane. A nonsymmetrical figure lends itself to a clear interpretation of whether the image has been rotated, reflected, or translated.

Next, I reviewed the transformations we were going to be performing with the crane. I placed a transparency of the coordinate axis on the overhead projector and placed my bird (still facing to the right and lying on its side) in Quadrant I of the coordinate axis (see next page). I said, "Here is our flattened crane." If we reflect it over the *y*-axis, what will it look like?"

Angela said, "It flips so that the head is looking to the west instead of to the east."

"What if we put it back in Quadrant One and rotate it over the *x*-axis?" I continued.

"It would be upside down," several students replied.

Joe added, "It kind of looks like the crane seeing its reflection in a pond."

"Very interesting connection!" I commented. "What if we translated the crane by moving it to the left and down?"

"It would be in a different spot, but facing the same way," Taquita said.

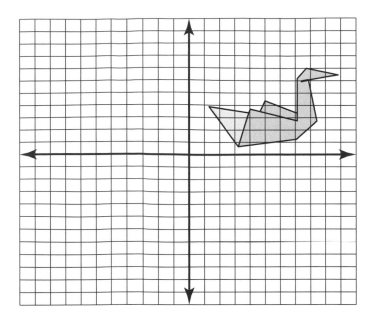

"What if I rotated the crane by ninety degrees?" I asked.

"It would turn," Brian said.

"Elaborate on that, Brian," I probed.

Brian approached the overhead and illustrated how the crane would turn and be sideways. He turned it so that it rotated into Quadrant IV, as shown below.

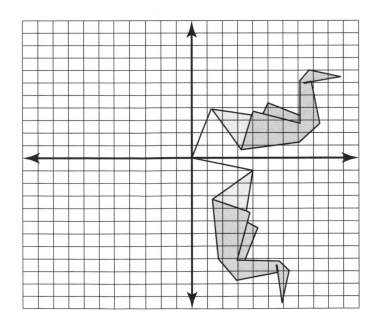

"Remember with rotations, we need to know where our point of rotation is so that we can rotate at that point. Brian has picked the origin as his point of rotation," I added.

I said to the class, "These transformations are called *rigid* transformations. Why are they called rigid?"

Stephanie said, "Because the shape of the crane doesn't change."

"What do you mean it doesn't change?" I probed.

Miranda raised her hand and said, "Well the position can move, but the shape itself doesn't change. So, the crane will be the same shape even after it's been moved."

I agreed, "Yes, the shape of our bird is the same as we move it around."

I modeled for students how to mark the points that made the vertices of the bird and then connect the dots. Students could now see the preimage (original position) of the crane on the transparency even when the bird was lifted from the grid. With student input, I labeled the coordinates of the bird's vertices with letters and then wrote the coordinates in a list.

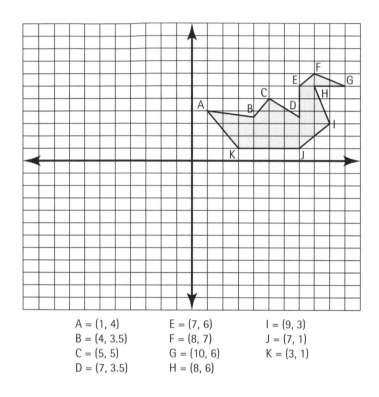

A = (1, 4) E = (7, 6) I = (9, 3)
B = (4, 3.5) F = (8, 7) J = (7, 1)
C = (5, 5) G = (10, 6) K = (3, 1)
D = (7, 3.5) H = (8, 6)

Next, I explained to students that they would be doing two reflections: one over the *y*-axis and one over the *x*-axis. As they worked, they were to think about and be ready to share a rule for how the coordinate pairs were affected by each reflection. I wrote the following on the board:

How will reflections affect the coordinate pairs of a figure?

What patterns do you notice with coordinate pairs when you

1. *reflect the crane over the y-axis?*
2. *reflect the crane over the x-axis?*

I replaced the crane in Quadrant I and asked students, "What will I do as a first step in exploring Question One?"

Many hands went up. Samuel replied, "You are going to flip it backwards, to the left." I asked him to come up and show me what he meant. He came to the overhead, picked up the bird, flipped it over the *y*-axis, set it down, and returned to his seat.

I asked the rest of the class, "Is this OK?"

Taquita said, "Does it matter where it goes in Quadrant Two, or does it just have to be backwards?"

"Great question," I said. "What is the answer?"

"It can go anywhere, as long as it is lined up," Felipe offered.

"I think it has to be the same distance from the *y*-axis," Celina stated.

I asked students to think about these two points: "For a reflection, does the object need to be lined up, straight? Does the position have to be exact?"

"It has to be exact," Jeremy chimed in, "because the *y*-axis is like a mirror. If we fold the paper on the *y*-axis, it has to match up." To model the last idea, I folded the transparency over the *y*-axis, traced the bird, and opened the transparency to show what a reflection would look like.

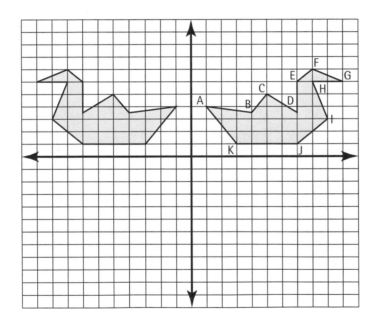

The class was quiet. I asked if the students agreed and they all did. I asked, "Can someone explain the next reflection?"

Brian said, "So if you reflect over *y*, it will be backwards. If you reflect over *x*, it will be upside down. So if we do the two, will it be in the third quadrant?"

I clarified that each time they did a reflection, they needed to start with the preimage, or original image, in Quadrant I. Then I said to the class, "This raises a good question. If we perform two transformations, one over each axis, what would the image in Quadrant Three look like? Would it be the same if we went to Quadrant Two first as it would be if we went to Quadrant Four first?" The students weren't sure. I suggested they start with the reflections into Quadrants II and IV and then see what happened if they reflected over the axis into Quadrant III.

I distributed the half-centimeter grid paper and reminded the students to record all of their coordinate pairs and to keep looking for relationships between the preimage and the new image they were making. I asked them to let me know if they thought they saw a relationship.

Because I thought some students would confuse the *x*-axis and *y*-axis, I labeled a rough sketch on my transparency that showed that the bird reflected over the *y*-axis was in Quadrant II and the one reflected over the *x*-axis was in Quadrant IV.

Observing the Students

Students worked in pairs with the half-centimeter coordinate axis, picking one of the birds they had made and using it to do each transformation. One pair of students was sketching the original bird in Quadrant I. One student asked, "What do we do with the vertices that don't end up on an exact point?" I responded that they could round to the nearest half unit. Another student wanted to know if the tip of the wings should be represented with one point, a flat line, or two points:

Another pair of students had flipped the crane and were recording points, but their bird was crooked. I asked, "If the original bird has a vertex at the point (one, six), then what should the position be after flipping it?"

Karissa said, "The opposite."

Her teammate, Hannah, added, "It would also be six high, but on the other side."

"So it would be (negative one, six)?" Karissa asked as she moved her bird to be on that coordinate and recorded the point.

I asked the group members how they might check if they were doing the reflection accurately. They each took their coordinate axis and folded it to see if the points in Quadrants I and II matched up.

We decided that it would be fine to do any of these sketches, as long as the original bird and its images had the same shape, since we were doing rigid transformations. We agreed it would not be OK if the original image had one point and the reflection had a flat line. Some of the students who were having trouble finding the points by using their bird decided to make a template of the bird, creating a flat image. They traced the bird onto colored paper and cut it out.

I reminded students to consider where the points were in Quadrant I as they worked on their sketches. Some students labeled the points with the coordinate pair. Others numbered the vertices and then recorded the coordinate pairs in a list they made in Quadrant III.

As I observed, I could see that some pairs continued to discuss and compare what coordinates they recorded and some pairs worked more independently. A number of the students continued to use the crane as a guide to make sure they were placing each point in the correct place in the new quadrant.

Amanda used a ruler to make sure the distance from the axis was the same for each reflected point. To do the transformation over the y-axis, she placed her ruler at the height of the vertex and then counted the number of lines to get to the new point and marked the spot. She continued this until she was finished with all the coordinate pairs.

Jackson did not use a ruler to plot the points but counted the vertical lines and then used the bird as a check to see that the shape was still preserved.

After students completed their sketches, several started to enter their data into their graphing calculators. I stopped the class for a moment and encouraged all students to do this only after they had finished all the recording of their reflections over each axis. The Stat Plot feature allows the student to program the calculator to assign Plot 1 so that L1 and L2 are x and y coordinates, Plot 2 so that L3 and L4 are x and y coordinates, and Plot 3 so that L5 and L6 are x and y coordinates. They entered the x and y values for the original bird in columns L1 and L2, then entered the coordinates of the bird that was reflected over the y-axis in L3 and L4, and, lastly, entered the coordinates of the bird reflected over the x-axis in L5 and L6 (the last two steps could have been switched).

The calculators enabled students to confirm that the coordinates they had recorded in fact would preserve the bird's shape and be reflected appropriately. (See Figures 11–1 through 11–3.)

A Class Discussion

I asked students to explain what they noticed about the coordinates when they reflected the bird over the y-axis. Students looked at their series of coordinates. Aaron said, "The y stays the same and the x value is the opposite."

"When does y stay the same?" I asked for clarification.

Aaron replied, "When it is flipped over the y-axis, the y stays the same."

"Why is this?" I asked. "Talk to your partner for a minute."

After students had some time to pair share, I asked the question again.

Figure 11–1: One student's reflection.

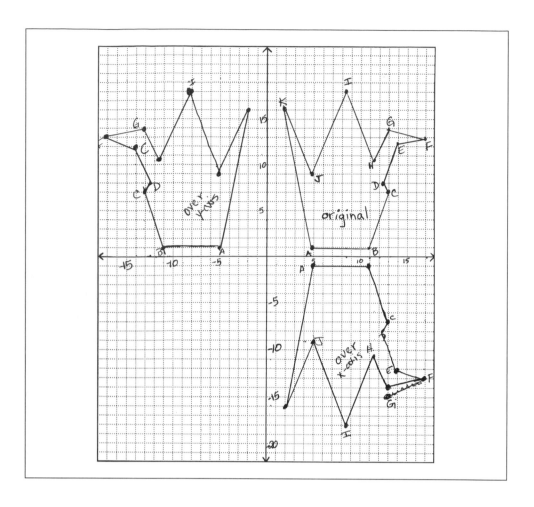

Figure 11–2: Coordinates for the reflections in Figure 11–1.

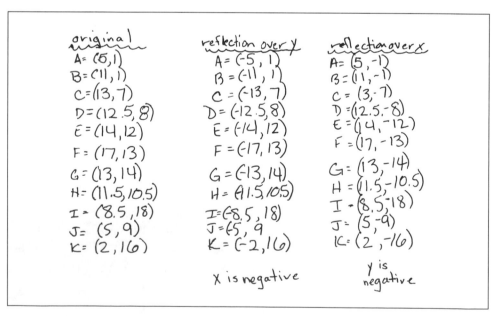

Katrina said, "It is because, if you take one point, like the beak, it is the same y, the same height; you are really just moving to a new x."

I asked, "Does anyone else have another way to explain this?"

Math and Nonfiction, Grades 6–8

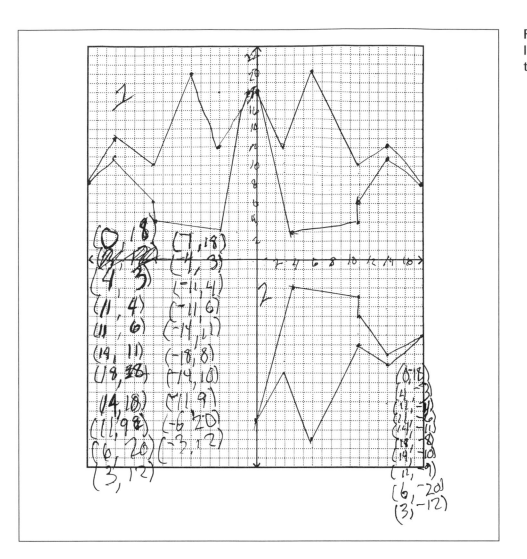

Figure 11–3: This student listed all his coordinates on the graph.

Amanda, who had used a ruler, said, "It's like placing the ruler parallel to the *x*-axis and then finding the point on the other side of the *y*-axis, so the *y* doesn't change—it's the same."

I asked students to record what this meant in algebraic terms. I wrote on the board:

Reflecting over the y-axis:

$$(x, y) \longrightarrow \underline{\hspace{2cm}}$$

Trevor offered, "It would be negative *x* and *y*." I recorded:

$$(x, y) \longrightarrow (-x, y)$$

I asked partners to talk this over and see if they agreed. In pairs, there was some discussion about which coordinate became negative, but they confirmed Trevor was correct by looking at their own data.

"What about reflecting over the *x*-axis?" I asked. "Work with a partner and look at your reflections over the *x*-axis and let me know what you think the reflection rule is and how you would record it algebraically."

As I walked around the room, I saw that students readily noticed that the x had remained the same and the y value was the opposite. Modeling after the reflection over the y-axis, students recorded:

$$(x, y) \longrightarrow (x, -y)$$

I asked, "How can your rules be used if we were to do this task again?"

At first the students were not sure what I was asking, but then Amanda said, "We wouldn't need to draw the pictures for the reflections; we could just use the rules and find the new coordinates."

This was an aha moment for several students, who said, "You mean we could have used this rule instead of drawing?!" I reminded them, while pointing at the instructions on the board, that I had started the lesson by encouraging them to keep their eyes out for a pattern that could help them find the coordinates for a reflection. It was a nice opportunity to reinforce that keeping our eyes out for rules or generalizations can help us solve problems more efficiently.

Telling Time

Telling Time, by Patricia J. Murphy (2007), is a book that describes the history of keeping time, including the progression of tools used to keep time, ranging from the sundial to the modern wristwatch.

In this lesson, focusing on patterns, measurement, and data analysis, students explore how the swing of a pendulum can be used to measure time. They find the periods of pendulums of various lengths to better understand how the rate of swing is dependent of the length of the pendulum. As students experiment, they collect data, create graphs, and draw conclusions.

MATERIALS

washers, all the same size, 3 per small group of students and 3 for the teacher

large paper clips, 1 per small group of students and 1 for the teacher

standard pencils, 1 per small group of students and 1 for the teacher

string, cut to different lengths ranging from 30 to 60 centimeters in increments of 5 centimeters, 1 per small group of students and 1 for the teacher

masking tape, several pieces per small group of students and a few for the teacher

meter sticks, 1 per small group of students and 1 for the teacher

Telling Time **record sheets,** 1 per student (see Blackline Masters)

overhead transparency of *Telling Time* **record sheet**

Introducing the Investigation

To begin the lesson, I explained to the students that the focus of this activity was going to be the swing of the pendulum used in early mechanical clocks and how it measures time. The book *Telling Time* is short, so I read the entire book to the class. When I was done, I reread pages 16 and 17, which describe the swing of the pendulum and its accuracy.

Generally, pendulums have been used in clocks for hundreds of years because the motion is so regular. In a grandfather clock, every time the pendulum swings back and forth, it moves a gear one notch. The gear then moves the hands of the clock. The length of the pendulum can be adjusted slightly if the clock is running too fast or slow.

The next step was to give students a little background knowledge. We discussed the following basics about a pendulum. A simple pendulum is made up of a rod or wire attached to a base at a pivot point. On the other end of the rod or wire is a weight (or bob). When moved to the side and released, the weight will swing back and forth because of gravity. Measuring this back-and-forth movement can be done in two ways: the frequency and the period. The *frequency* of the pendulum is how many times it goes back and forth per second. The *period* of the pendulum is how long it takes for it to go back and forth one time. The *swing rate,* the focus of this activity, is how many times the pendulum goes back and forth in thirty seconds.

I explained to the students that they were going to build a pendulum with a piece of string, a pencil, a paper clip, and some washers, and that they would collect data about the pendulum and its swing rate. I put students in groups of three and assigned students to the roles of materials manager, recorder, and time keeper. The materials manager was asked to pick up three washers, a paper clip, a pencil, a length of string, several pieces of tape, a meter stick, and three *Telling Time* record sheets.

I showed the students how to build the pendulum. I bent a paper clip into an S shape, tied a piece of string to one end of the paper clip, and hung three washers on the other end. I told students they had to be careful to try to all tie their clips as close to the end of the string as possible, in order to preserve the length of string. I taped a pencil to my desk so that one end hung over the edge. Then I wrapped the loose end of the string once around the end of the pencil hanging over the edge and used tape to hold it in place. Finally, I tested the pendulum to see that it would swing freely back and forth without hitting the desk.

After all groups had made their pendulums, I showed an overhead transparency of the table that the students would be completing and explained that they would record their information on the overhead to share it with the class. They would need to copy the data from the overhead onto their own table to have a complete set of data for various string lengths.

PENDULUM SWING Data Collection				
String length	30 sec. swing rate Trial #1	30 sec. swing rate Trial #2	30 sec. swing rate Trial #3	30 sec. swing rate Average
32	25	25	25	25
50	20	20	20	20
70	17	17	17	17
60	18	18	18	18
11	40	42	40	40
20	30	30	30	30

Figure 12–1: Set of class data for pendulum experiment.

Next, I modeled how to do the experiment. I demonstrated how to measure the length of the pendulum with a meter stick from the pencil to the bottom of the weights and then instructed each group to do the same. I had the recorder from each group write the measurement on the board. I pulled the weight so that it was tight and almost parallel to the floor. I modeled how to use the clock to time the pendulum for thirty seconds as soon as I released it. I counted the number of full swings in thirty seconds. I then instructed the time keeper from each group to time the group's pendulum for thirty seconds while the other group members counted the number of full swings. The students pulled their pendulums back and released them. They counted the number of full swings and recorded the number of swings for their group on the overhead. I explained that the total number of swings in the given time (thirty seconds) was called the *swing rate*.

I directed the groups to repeat the experiment two more times to make sure that they measured the time and counted the swings accurately. I instructed them to release the pendulum at the same angle, or from the same place, each time. I asked the students to find the mean swing rate to share with the class. The rest of these numbers were recorded on the overhead. (See Figure 12–1.)

A Class Discussion

We then had a discussion regarding the wide variety of swing rates that were collected.

I asked the class, "Why didn't each group have the same swing rate?"

Sue answered, "You can tell from the table that we have different string lengths."

"It looks like longer strings had a less of a swing rate," added Bob.

"Why is that?" I asked.

"Well, I think it is because the string is longer so the pendulum has a longer way to go when it swings, so it takes longer to get back and forth," John answered.

"The swing rates could also be different because we may not have all dropped it from the same height," Joan suggested.

"We kind of played around with that while we were waiting in between trials, and I don't think it really makes that much of a difference," Sue replied.

"That is an interesting idea and something we should experiment with more. It is also the reason I asked you to be consistent and release from the same height each time. We can look into that during our next class," I said.

"Maybe it was the weight that made the difference," suggested Paul.

Sue clarified, "We all had the same weights."

"Well, let's see if we can find a pattern by graphing the data we've collected about the string length," I said.

I had each student graph the class data on the bottom of the record sheet with string length on the *x*-axis and the swing rate on the *y*-axis. (See Figure 12–2.) I asked the students to describe any patterns that they noticed. They were able to conclude that the shorter the string, the greater the swing rate.

I followed up by asking students to use the graph to predict the swing rate for a string length of 80 centimeters and other measurements not recorded in their table.

Figure 12–2: The graph of class data showed the swing rates decreased as the string length increased.

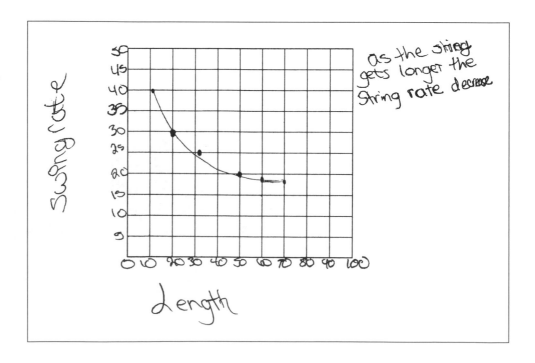

Math and Nonfiction, Grades 6–8

We had one final discussion about what other changes they could make in the pendulums that might affect the swing rate.

Dan suggested, "We could change the number of washers."

"How would we do that?" I probed.

"We could start with one washer and continue adding the washers but leave our string the same length and test the swing rate with different number of washers," explained Rachel.

"We could also see if the angle we drop it from makes a difference," Andrea suggested.

I told the students we would test some of these ideas in future classes.

Extensions

- Continue with other experiments, such as trying washers that are smaller or larger than the ones in this experiment.

- Have students attempt to make a pendulum that swings a specific number of times, for example, ask them to find the length of string that will make the pendulum swing exactly ten times in thirty seconds.

Summary

Following the extensions, lead a discussion to summarize what students have learned. Following are some of the important ideas they should talk about:

- The swing rate, and also the frequency, of a pendulum is dependent on the length of the string or wire. The shorter the wire, the greater the swing rate. Longer pendulums swing with a slower swing rate and therefore have a longer period.

- The swing rate, and also the frequency, of a pendulum is independent of the mass of the bob. In other words, changing the weight does not affect the swing rate of the pendulum. A pendulum with a heavy bob will move at the same rate as one with a lighter bob. This will make sense if students understand that the acceleration of gravity on a falling object is independent of the mass of the object.

- The swing rate, and also the frequency, of a pendulum is independent of the amplitude of the swing, provided the initial angle is not large. At larger angles, there is a slight change in the swing rate. Changing the starting angle of the pendulum (how far you pull it to the side before releasing it) has only a very slight effect on the swing rate.

Additional Ideas

200% of Nothing

An Eye-Opening Tour Through the Twists and Turns of Math Abuse and Innumeracy

A. K. Dewdney's delightful book *200% of Nothing* (1993) presents kid-friendly explanations of the many ways that numbers are twisted and statistics are turned to mislead the common person. Topics include statistical abuse in government, politics, finance, advertising, and the media, to name a few. The examples are real, provided by readers of *Scientific American*, a journal in which the author has a column. This book is an excellent tool for showing the power of mathematics in the real world and illustrating the importance of being mathematically literate in today's society.

Because the entire book is filled with uses and misuses of mathematics, it offers many ideas for doing middle school mathematics related to the real world. Here, we share an activity about counting people that employs set theory (union and intersection of sets). Then we briefly mention three other opportunities: (1) manipulating percent increase and percent decrease facts to make it look like there are gains when there aren't; (2) finding the mathematical errors of advertisements that use data out of context; and (3) calculating compound interest using car sales.

MATERIALS

Venn diagram templates, 1 per pair of students (see Blackline Masters)

optional: sticky notes, 1 per student

The Investigation

The introduction of *200% of Nothing* is worth sharing with students. They themselves need to recognize "math abuse." Chapter 1 offers several innumeracy examples, one of which is "Death by Aftermath" (page 6). One coroner counted fifty deaths after the 1965 Gulf Coast hurricane Betsy, but a TV reporter counted ninety-three. When asked how the studio counted ninety-three, he said the studio collected numbers from the police, the fire department, the Coast Guard, and so on, and added them to the number from the morgue. After reading to this point in the text, stop and ask students what they think happened. Students may have several explanations that are possible, but focus their attention on the notion of people being counted more than once. Ask students to work with a partner and use the Venn diagram template to figure out a possible way this could have happened with reports from only the fire department, the Coast Guard, and the morgue.

Before students begin working with their partners, draw a three-circle Venn diagram on the board and place a 2 in the middle section. Ask, "How many would the morgue count?" (Two) Ask, "How many would the fire department count?" (Two) Ask, "How many would the Coast Guard count?" (Two) Finally, ask, "How many would the TV reporter count?" (Six since two were reported by each of the three groups).

Now put a number in the overlap between only two circles, indicating people that were double counted, and ask the same questions. Repeat with several more numbers in different locations on the diagram.

Once partners have prepared their Venn diagrams, ask each pair to exchange with another pair of students to check the counting. (See Figure 13–1.)

Figure 13–1: This pair of students' Venn diagram showed a possible solution of 93 for the TV reporter's count.

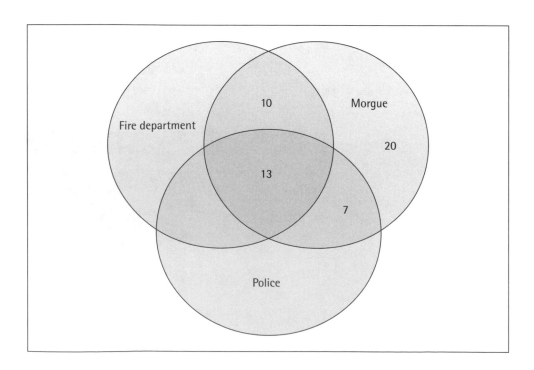

Math and Nonfiction, Grades 6-8

Questions to ask students might include:

- How many bodies were counted by the fire department? The Coast Guard?

- How many bodies had not yet arrived at the morgue?

To reverse and extend this investigation, create a Venn diagram on the board with three categories such as Have a Brother, Have Brown Eyes, and Wearing Jeans. Ask students to place an *X* for a sticky note in the Venn diagram where it is true for them. (See Figure 13–2.)

Once the data are placed, ask students "how many people" questions, such as "How many people have brown eyes?", starting with each individual section. Record totals for each category on the whiteboard or overhead. Then ask questions that involve "and" situations, such as "How many people have brown eyes, are wearing jeans, *and* have a brother?" or "How many people have brown eyes *and* are wearing jeans?" In this second example, students are likely to debate if the middle section should count.

Encourage students to provide a justification for yes or no answers. In fact, the middle section *should* be included because the people in the middle section do have brown eyes and are wearing jeans; they just also have a brother. One way to help students see this is to ask those

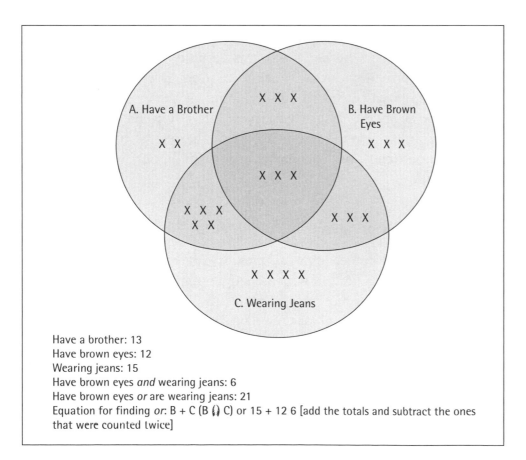

Figure 13–2: Venn diagram of class data.

Have a brother: 13
Have brown eyes: 12
Wearing jeans: 15
Have brown eyes *and* wearing jeans: 6
Have brown eyes *or* are wearing jeans: 21
Equation for finding *or*: B + C (B {} C) or 15 + 12 6 [add the totals and subtract the ones that were counted twice]

that have brown eyes and are wearing jeans to stand. Some will have brothers and some won't.

Next, ask "or" questions, such as "How many people have brown eyes *or* are wearing jeans?" Ask students to explain their counting strategies. If the students are in algebra, or preparing for algebra, see if they can determine a way to figure out the *or* question, using the information they have already recorded so that they don't have to count all the people again. They might notice that they can count the number for each separate circle and subtract the overlap. The equations are often found in formal Algebra I texts in the chapter on sets, but are very difficult for students to understand.

If time allows and/or students need more experience, have small groups of students create their own categories in a Venn diagram, collect data from their classmates, and respond to questions similar to those above.

Another example of misleading counting is reported in "Drunk, Drugged, Depressed, and Dangerous!" on page 11.

Additional Problems

Percent Increase and Percent Decrease

Read the opening two paragraphs in "Instant Wealth and Rebounding Grades" (on page 9). Ask students to provide a mathematical explanation of this situation. Then read the next paragraph and ask students to predict whether the scores actually were better or worse than they were previously. This is a good problem-solving task where students will need to supply some of their own numbers to explore the problem, or use variables. After they have investigated it, have groups share their reports. Read the rest of the story. Have students create their own scenarios that sound good but are not (or vice versa).

The Mathematics of Advertising (Chapter 3)

Chapter 3 offers numerous examples of advertisements that have a logical vacuum—"a void in which a single number or fact floats without any frame of reference" (44). Read some or all of these to the class. For each one that you read, ask students to consider what is missing or flawed in the advertisement.

Have students find additional examples on their own from TV, newspapers, or the Internet. This can be an ongoing project where examples are posted on a bulletin board and discussed as time allows. This can go a long way in increasing students' capacity as consumers of knowledge and products!

"The Irrelevant Fund," a car sales example on pages 11–13, well illustrates "compound blindness." This is an opportunity for students to explore compound interest and consider options in purchasing a car.

Present the scenario to the class, including all the numerical information. Tell the story in your own words, or read pages 12 and 13. Ask students, in pairs or small groups, to discuss the reasoning of both the salesman and the detective until they are able to explain which plan is better and why. Spreadsheet software would be an excellent tool here. When everyone is ready, lead a class discussion.

Finally, provide students with current interest rates for a car dealership and a savings account and have them determine the best decision for today's car purchaser.

The All-New Book of Lists for Kids

Sandra and Harry Choron's *All-New Book of Lists for Kids* (2002) contains hundreds of lists on a wide range of topics from helping people seek careers to interesting websites. Some of the topics are useful to middle school students, such as "Nine Ways to Improve Your Memory" (45) and "Ten Jobs You'll Enjoy if You Like Being Outdoors" (58). Many of the topics provide fun and interesting trivia, such as "The Ten Most Popular Fast Foods" (203) and "William Shatner Lists Three Things About *Star Trek* That He Wishes Were Real" (319). Many of the lists can be used for a statistics investigation, comparing class data with the data in the book.

This lesson, integrating number, algebra, and data, uses the list "Toy Prices, 1897" as a context for exploring costs then and now. Provided with the 1897 prices of various toys, students analyze data and use proportional reasoning to find what the prices should be today, taking into consideration the rate of inflation. They then compare the projected prices to the actual prices of today and report their findings, including the percent of increase or decrease for each toy.

MATERIALS

toy prices record sheets, 1 per student (see Blackline Masters)

The Investigation

To begin this lesson, you may want to read several lists from the book. Ask students what toys they have liked playing with over the years. Then share with them the list of toys and prices from 1897 on pages 133–34. Distribute the record sheets.

Ask students if they think that toys were easy for families to buy back then, given those prices, and why. Students may argue yes or no. Explain to students that they are going to figure out if today's prices are relatively cheaper or relatively more expensive. As a first step, tell them that they will need to do some research on the current price of these toys (this can be done prior to or during this lesson). If you have computers with Internet access, ask students to search online to find the current price of three of the toys listed in the table. If you don't have access to computers, there are several other options: students can look at home for prices, you can provide toy catalogs, or you can provide the prices for them.

Once students have collected current prices, ask them to consider inflation, or the increase in the price of everything over the years. Share with students the following data, downloaded from the NASA website (http://cost.jsc.nasa.gov), which links to various inflation sites, including *The Inflation Calculator* (www.westegg.com/inflation):

What cost $1.00 in 1897 would cost $24.61 in 2007. If you were to buy exactly the same products in 2007 and 1897, they would cost you $1.00 and $0.04 respectively.

Ask students to use this data to figure out if the current prices of their three chosen toys are better or worse than the prices in 1897. Students may choose to use the price from 1897 and see what it would be now, or they may choose the current price and figure out what that would have cost in 1897. Ask students to share their results and how they found them.

Next, ask students to report on the percent of increase or decrease of the price of the toy. Here is an example:

Spalding Official Boys' League Baseball, 1897 = $0.72

Using proportional reasoning, this item would have cost $17.72 in 2007. A quick search on the Web showed the best price in 2007 to be a Wilson Boys' League Baseball at $25.99. Therefore, the price was more expensive in 2007 than it should have been. In fact it was a percent increase of 47 percent!

The Breakfast Cereal Gourmet

The Breakfast Cereal Gourmet, by David Hoffman (2005), even looks like a cereal box! It is full of interesting historical facts about different kinds of cereals. The section "(Snap, Crackle) Pop Goes the Culture," beginning on page 7, is a walk down memory lane. It offers information about the creation and consumption of cereals, including those that have disappeared or have been replaced. The majority of the book contains recipes made with cereals. Each is accompanied by a story of a famous restaurant that uses that recipe or a fact about that particular cereal. This is a wonderful book!

This geometry and measurement lesson is about designing cereal boxes that are environmentally friendly and practical. Students determine the surface area and volume of rectangular prisms as well as other three-dimensional shapes. To physically create the boxes, students need to understand that a variety of nets can form a shape, a challenging concept for many.

MATERIALS

miniboxes of cereal, all the same size, 1 per small group of students

inch grid paper, 2 sheets per student (see Blackline Masters)

rulers, 1 or 2 per small group of students

overhead transparency or class chart listing volume and surface area formulas for three-dimensional shapes

class chart listing instructions for creating cereal boxes (see page 110)

36-by-48-inch poster board, 1 piece per small group of students

cereal box evaluation handouts, 1 per student (see Blackline Masters)

Note: This lesson is best done as a two- to three-day exploration or in an extended class period.

Preparing for the Lesson

Ahead of time, prepare some questions to ask the class based on information found on pages 7 to 21 in the book. Here are some suggestions:

Cereal Numbers

1. How many bowls of cereal does the average person consume in one year?

2. What are the top three grocery store items (in order) on which Americans spend their money?

3. How many pounds of sugar are used per year in the cereal industry?

4. What mineral is added to cereal to increase its nutritional value?

5. Which cereal has the most sugar?

6. What cereal was removed from the stores because when children ate the cereal, it made their poop turn pink?

The Investigation

Begin the lesson by asking students to predict the answers to the questions you prepared. Next read aloud the passages from pages 7–21 that provide the answers to the questions. In addition, show the class the time line on pages 2–3. Students will find this interesting. In one class, my students got a kick out of the story of Dr. John Kellogg, a director at a sanitarium, who invented granola and then abandoned his creation. The story concludes by saying Kellogg turned his attention to nuts ("What kind of nuts?" students asked!). They also enjoyed the story of the recall of Franken Berry cereal (21), the story of how Wheaties came to be (96–97), and several others.

Show students the cover of the book and ask why they think cereal boxes are shaped the way they are. After some sharing, ask students if they think the design of the cereal boxes that they are familiar with is the most environmentally friendly way to package cereal. Say, "In other words, what shape of box can use the least cardboard and hold the most cereal?"

Place students in groups of three to four. Distribute the miniboxes of cereal, the inch grid paper, rulers, and scissors to student groups.

Instruct each student to draw a flat pattern of the minibox on the grid paper, *without cutting the box open*. Explain that this is called a *net*. Ask students to calculate the surface area and the volume of their box using inches and to write the steps they took to solve the problem and/or show their work. Have the list of formulas available for students to use.

After about ten minutes, ask students to share their findings. Once they have discussed (and possibly debated) the nets, surface area, and volume, instruct each group to cut open its box with scissors so it stays in one piece and lays flat, thus creating a net. Have students compare their flattened box with their drawings and see if they want to make any changes to their drawings or calculations if they want to.

Tell students that today they are going to be graphic designers. Explain that each group will design a cereal box of any shape that is environmentally friendly (holds the maximum amount of cereal with the least amount of poster board) and can hold 300 cubic inches. Let the students know that they can, like the label on the cover of the book says, "think outside the box," hinting that they can, for example, create a cylindrical or cubic container. Explain that once complete, each container will be judged by the group's classmates according to the following criteria: rationale for the design, accuracy, neatness, attractiveness, and clarity of presentation.

Post and discuss the following instructions for the project.

1. Together as a group, pick a shape for your cereal box and determine its dimensions. The box must be environmentally friendly and hold 300 cubic inches.

2. Each member should sketch the net that can fold into your group's box on his or her own grid paper.

3. As a group, carefully draw the net you sketched on your poster board.

4. Cut out the net, fold it into a box, and tape it.

5. Find the volume and surface area of your box.

6. Add a name to your cereal box and decorate it.

7. Prepare your presentation.

Emphasize to the groups that they will receive only one piece of poster board, and the net—*one* flat pattern—must eventually fold into a container that holds cereal. Careful planning is needed. Make available the list of formulas for three-dimensional shapes so that students don't have to spend time looking through their book for the formulas. Once there are no more questions, let the class begin working. As you observe students, watch for those who choose a cylinder. Their net *may* become three distinct pieces when cut. Let them know that it is OK if this happens. Groups' presentations can be as simple as giving two-minute reports on the decisions they made and the measurements of their product or as grand as preparing an advertisement for their cereal box. Students may even want to record their advertisement at home on a video and then show it to the class. This is an ideal opportunity to collaborate with a speech, drama, or English teacher.

After each group's presentation, distribute the evaluation handout and ask students to rate the presentation. Consider giving the highest-scoring boxes blue ribbons or showcasing them in some other way.

Gutsy Girls
Young Women Who Dare

Gutsy Girls, by Tina Schwager and Michele Schuerger (1999), is a chapter book filled with true stories of twenty-five brave, determined, and hard-working girls and young women who have performed daring feats.

In this algebra investigation, students graph the adventure of rock climber Beth Rodden based on the descriptive account of her climb. This investigation enables students to explore how various rates of change are presented in a graph.

MATERIALS

centimeter grid paper, 1 sheet per student (see Blackline Masters)

The Investigation

"Beth Rodden, Rock Climber" (62–68) is a chapter that can be read aloud in five to ten minutes to set the stage for this investigation. Read the chapter and discuss Beth's climb with the students. Explain that they are going to make a graph to illustrate how Beth's height above the ground changed over time. Discuss the events of the climb as a class. Pass out the grid paper and ask the students what labels belong on the *x*-axis and *y*-axis of the graph based on the event. They should conclude that *Time* will be on the *x*-axis and *Height Above the Ground* will be on the *y*-axis. Ask the students what they need to know in order to number the axes. Most likely, several volunteers will suggest the total height of the rock as well as the total time for the climb. If no one remembers the exact height, reread the first paragraph on page 63. It tells the reader, "The cliff ascends about fifty feet."

The time it took to make the climb isn't clear, so students will have to use an estimate of the amount of time (approximately thirty minutes).

Reread part of the story, beginning in the middle of page 64 with the words "At first," and continue reading to the end. Have students record "events" that they should consider when making the graph. When you are done, have students share to be sure that everyone has a list of all the major events. The list should contain the following: the first six moves were extremely difficult; Beth reached a rest point but didn't pause long; she got through the next ten moves quickly; she stopped at a small break to chalk her hand; she took two more moves; she rested again; and then she threw herself up. Finally she was lowered on the rope down the cliff.

Tell each student to roughly sketch on the grid paper what he thinks the climb would look like. Have students share with a partner and adjust if they feel it is necessary.

Read the part about the climb again and have students follow the line they created as they listen to the story. After rereading, ask the following questions:

- How does your graph compare with the story?

- Do you feel it is an accurate depiction of the climb? Explain.

- How does your graph compare with other students' graphs?

- Where did Beth move the slowest? What does the graph look like at this point?

- Where did Beth move the fastest? What does the graph look like?

- How many times and where did Beth rest? What does the graph look like at those points?

- How does Beth's descent compare with her ascent?

The History of Everyday Life

The History of Everyday Life, by Elaine Landau (2006), gives a historical account of major inventions that changed how we live. The book consists of topics many students have experience with and one item in particular they use every day—the toilet! The focus of this lesson is on "Indoor Plumbing" (Chapter 2). Environmental issues of water conservation can be discussed before and after this investigation.

In this lesson, focusing on number and data analysis, students create circle graphs to illustrate the use of water in urban settings. They change percentages into degrees to create the graphs and determine what percent residential toilet use is of total water usage.

MATERIALS

protractors, 1 per student
compasses, 1 per student

The Investigation

Begin by reading aloud pages 14 through 21 of The History of Everyday Life, which trace the history of indoor plumbing, from chamber pots to the outhouse to the modern toilet. After reading, ask students what problems were solved through the invention of the modern toilet. (It reduced the spread of diseases such as typhoid fever, cholera, and dysentery. It also made cities smell better!) Ask the students, "While the toilet was a great invention, what new problems has it caused?" They will most likely suggest that toilets use a great deal of water and produce a great deal of wastewater.

According to the Environmental Protection Agency (EPA), "Residential demands account for about three-fourths of the total urban water demand. Indoor use accounts for roughly 60 percent of all residential use, and of this, toilets (at 3.5 gallons per flush) use nearly 40 percent. Toilets, showers, and faucets combined represent two-thirds of all indoor water use" (http://vdh.state.va.us/Environmental Health/Onsite/GMP/Attachments/GMP119-WCR.pdf). The impact of residential toilets on total urban water use is still hard to understand after following that series of statistics. Pose this question to the class: "Exactly what percent of total urban water usage is represented by residential toilet use?"

The answer to this question can be better understood visually with pie graphs. Give each student several sheets of blank paper, a protractor, and a compass and ask students to make a pie graph to illustrate the total urban water demand, showing residential and commercial use. (See Figure 17–1.) While this can be done simply by using technology, when done by hand, circle graphs provide an opportunity for students to explore the relationship between percentages (based on 100) and angles (based on 360 degrees), a proportional reasoning activity.

Next, ask students to make a pie graph of residential water use, illustrating indoor and outdoor use. (See Figure 17–2.)

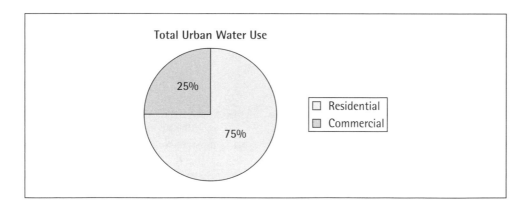

Figure 17–1: Pie graph illustrating residential and commercial use of water.

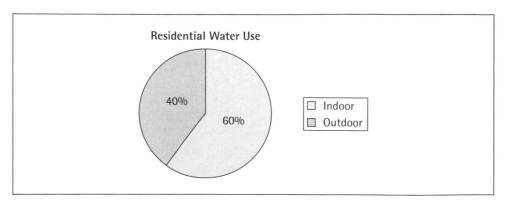

Figure 17–2: Pie graph illustrating residential indoor and outdoor use of water.

Third, ask students to make a pie graph of indoor water use. (See Figure 17–3.) Toilets use nearly 40 percent. Since toilets, showers, and faucets represent two-thirds, or 67 percent, showers and faucets represent 27 percent, and other, 33 percent.

After students have created their three representations, ask them to figure out what percent of residential water is used for residential toilets and draw the pie graph. (See Figure 17–4.) (Forty percent of 60 percent = 24 percent of residential water is used for residential toilets.) Discuss the concept of multiplying a part by a part, resulting in a smaller part.

Finally, ask students to find the percent of the total urban water supply used for residential toilets and draw the pie graph. (See Figure 17–5.)

Figure 17–3: Pie graph illustrating residential indoor use of water.

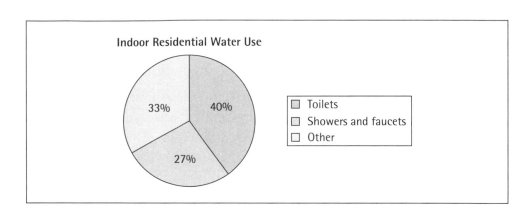

Figure 17–4: Pie graph illustrating percent of residential water used for toilets.

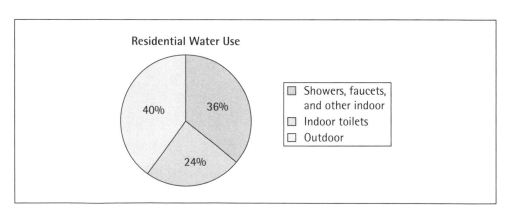

Figure 17–5: Pie graph illustrating percent of total urban water supply used for residential toilets.

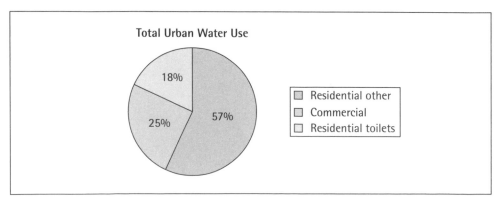

Math and Nonfiction, Grades 6–8

(Twenty-four percent of 75 percent = 18 percent of total urban water is used for residential toilets.)

Conclude the lesson by sharing some ways that water can be conserved, in particular through toilet use. Strategies include buying the types of toilets that use less water to flush each time, not flushing unnecessarily (some people flush other things down the toilet), and not flushing after "minor" use (wait for several uses).

If the World Were a Village

A Book About the World's People

In David J. Smith's beautifully illustrated *If the World Were a Village* (2002), each two-page spread presents proportional statistics about various aspects of the world if the world were just a village of one hundred people. For example, if the world's languages were represented in a village of one hundred people, then twenty-two people would speak Chinese, nine would speak English, and so on. Other topics include nationalities, ages, religion, food, and literacy. This book enables readers to develop a deeper understanding of the world in which we live, including important social issues. It explicitly focuses on cultural and geographic diversity.

In this activity, students create graphic displays of the data supplied in the book and use rational number equivalencies to describe the data. This book lends itself well to social studies and could be used for an integrated lesson.

MATERIALS

If the World Were a Village Topic Cards (see Blackline Masters)

centimeter grid paper, 2–3 sheets per small group of students (see Blackline Masters)

calculators, 1 per student

globe(s) or map(s) of the world, 1 for the class or 1 per small group of students

optional: computer with spreadsheet software

The Investigation

If the World Were a Village provides data about the world in a brief format, like the evening news. Ask students to imagine that they are going to be preparing a news brief that can appear on the nightly news or in the newspaper. Explain that as they listen to you read, they will need to focus on how they can represent the data in a meaningful way to their audience.

Read the book to the class. Each two-page spread is a stand-alone report of something in the global village. As you read the introductory paragraph for each spread, you may ask students to predict how the one hundred people will be divided into the subcategories for that topic. After reading the book, give each group of two to four students one topic card, which they must use to write their report.

Explain to students that they will be using the data you have given them to make a report. Their reports must include the following:

- A graphic display of the data (or two displays). Discuss what types of graphs they might use (pictographs, circle graphs, bar graphs). Ask students to create their graphic display using blank paper, centimeter grid paper, or spreadsheet software such as Excel.

  Remind students that the representation they pick should be the best way to show listeners or readers the distribution of their data. In addition, remind students that during their presentation, they should use the globe or map to help illustrate the location of the places about which they are reporting.

- A script that needs to include two mathematical pieces. First, fractions and percents must be used to describe the data. Suggest to students that they pick friendly fractions that will make sense to the common listener or reader. Second, write on the board the actual number of people in the real world for each subcategory, based on the population of the world.

Prior to starting the small-group work, collectively brainstorm how to most clearly communicate the data in fractions and percents. For example, the book states that twenty-two out of one hundred people speak a Chinese dialect in the global village. Rather than use $\frac{11}{50}$, the exact simplification of $\frac{22}{100}$, it is more helpful to say "slightly more than one-fifth of the population" or "almost one-fourth or twenty-five percent of the world's population."

Allow students to work in small groups for a designated time span to prepare both their graphs and their news reports. Once completed, have students present their work to the class.

If You Made a Million

In his classic style, David M. Schwartz develops the concept of one million around money in his book *If You Made a Million* (1989). The picture book begins with the reader earning a penny and works it way up to the reader earning a million dollars, illustrating equivalencies for each amount and what the amount might look like. In addition, saving and borrowing money are explored with a discussion of earning compound interest.

This book presents many possibilities for exploring mathematics, and several are discussed in the back of the book. The lesson here is drawn from the popular TV and movie situation when kidnappers demand that a ransom of one million dollars is delivered in a briefcase. The problem requires students to measure dollar bills to see how many of them will fit into a briefcase. Students cannot solve this problem with only division; they have to use proportional reasoning as well.

MATERIALS

briefcase

stack(s) of 20 one-dollar bills or 20 pieces of paper, each cut to the size of a one-dollar bill, at least 1

rulers, 1 per small group of students

calculators, 1 per student

overhead transparencies or sheets of newsprint, 1 per small group of students

The Investigation

Read *If You Made a Million* to the class. After reading, ask students if they remember how the book describes one million dollars. The book has an illustration of a tall stack of one-dollar bills. It also explains that the bill with the largest value made today is the one-hundred-dollar bill.

Launch the lesson by presenting the following problem, adapting it to a specific show or clip, if you like.

A kidnapper [from a popular TV series] asks for a million dollars in unmarked bills to be delivered to the trash can at the park. The parents go to the bank, take out one million dollars in twenty-dollar bills, and place the money in a briefcase. They then go to the park and put the briefcase in the trash can. The show goes to commercial. You are at the edge of your seat. "Is this actually possible?" you ask yourself. You're not wondering if the bribe will get the child back, but if the money can fit in the briefcase. Prepare a presentation that convinces us that the money can or cannot fit in the briefcase.

Hold up the model briefcase and a few one-dollar bills. Ask students to predict whether the one million dollars will fit in the briefcase or not. Record the vote on the board for later comparison with students' findings. After posing the problem, place students in groups of three or four. Ask them to think about all the information and the approach they will use to prove or disprove the validity of this situation. After about five minutes, ask students to share their ideas. These ideas might include that they will need to measure the size of a twenty-dollar bill, measure the height of a stack of bills, measure the size of the briefcase, and figure out how many twenty-dollar bills are needed to make one million dollars.

After students share their ideas, display the stack of money and have students assist in doing whatever measurements they believe are needed, recording the measurements on the board. Alternatively, if you have enough bills, students can measure the stacks in their groups. Also, have the class work together to measure the briefcase.

Remind students that their goal is to use math to prepare and illustrate an explanation that will convince the rest of the class that the money will or won't fit in the briefcase. Invite students to send a representative from their group to get any supplies they think they need, such as calculators.

If students finish early, ask them to explore the following extensions:

1. How big would a briefcase need to be to hold a million dollars in twenty-dollar bills?

2. Would one million dollars in hundred-dollar bills fit in the briefcase?

3. What would be the smallest briefcase that could hold one million dollars in one hundred–dollar bills?

When students are nearly finished, ask each group to prepare its report on newsprint or an overhead transparency. Allow each group an opportunity to present and explain how it figured out whether or not the twenty-dollar bills would fit in the briefcase. If students have had the chance to explore the extensions, ask them to share those results too. If they have not, ask students Question 2. This question can be answered without repeating the process of measuring and calculating if students recognize that the number of bills would be one-fifth of what they had in twenty-dollar bills. This can also be assigned as a homework investigation.

The Joy of π

The Joy of π, by David Blatner (1997), presents a concise history of pi, including major milestones in determining pi, the personality of pi, and interesting patterns found in pi. Throughout the book, almost like a border, in very tiny print, is pi itself, listed out to thousands if not millions of digits. There are numerous books on pi, but this one offers content that is appropriate for middle school students and can be easily incorporated into a lesson on pi. One of the milestones in approximating the relationship between the diameter and the area of a circle was a method developed by a Greek mathematician named Antiphon. He created larger and larger polygons inside a circle, found the area of each one, and judged the largest area to be about the same as the area of the circle. Two hundred years later, Archimedes picked up on this idea but focused on perimeter. It is his work that is the basis for this investigation.

This geometry lesson is an opportunity for students to place themselves in the position of the Greeks trying to find the circumference of a circle without using pi. Using Archimedes's idea, students find the perimeter of a hexagon and dodecagon inside and outside of a circle and calculate the average of the two measurements. The goals of this lesson are twofold: to accurately use angle and length measures and to gain a deeper understanding of what pi is and to understand why mathematicians have studied and refined the concept for thousands of years.

MATERIALS

approximating pi record sheets, 1 per student (see Blackline Masters)

rulers with inches marked in sixteenths, 1 per student

angle rulers or protractors, 1 per student

optional: *The Joy of π* additional circles, 1 set per student (see Blackline Masters)

optional: computer with geometric drawing software

Note: This lesson lends itself well to using electronic drawing tools, such as Geometer's Sketchpad or those found in a Microsoft Word program.

The Investigation

Ask students to share what they know about pi. List their ideas on the board or an overhead transparency. Ask students if they know when and how pi came into being. Students may not be aware of the long history of mathematicians trying to figure out the relationship between the diameter and the area (or circumference) of a circle. Ask students to think about how mathematicians years ago might have tried to figure out the relationship. Allow students to brainstorm ideas.

Read "A History of Pi: The Greeks," on pages 16–21, to the class. Tell students they are going to be approximating the circumference of circles without using pi.

Give each student an *Approximating Pi* record sheet, a ruler, and an angle ruler or protractor. Ask students to start with Circle A on the record sheet. Show students how to use the ruler or the angle ruler or protractor to inscribe a hexagon. Here are the steps for inscribing a hexagon in a circle:

1. A hexagon has six sides. Three hundred sixty degrees divided by six is 60 degrees, which means that if one creates six radii (or in this case three diameters) in the circle, each 60 degrees apart, the points where they hit the circumference will be the vertices of a hexagon.

2. Draw a diameter.

3. Use the protractor or angle ruler to rotate 60 degrees in the center of the circle and make another diameter.

4. Repeat this process one more time.

5. Mark a dot on the circumference of the circle where each diameter ends.

6. Connect the dots.

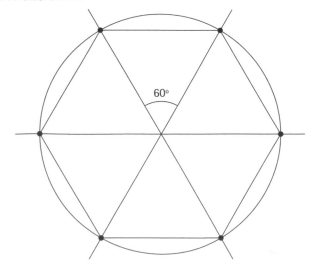

Once they have inscribed the hexagon, students can find the perimeter using a ruler. Ask students to work individually and then compare their measures with a partner. While this task can be more easily done in the metric system, using inches (and therefore fractions) better parallels the work of Archimedes because neither the decimal point nor zero had yet been invented. Once students have the perimeter, tell them to follow the same process and inscribe a dodecagon (a twelve-sided polygon) in the same circle. Since it has twice as many sides, they will need to have a diameter every 30 degrees. Because half are already drawn, students only need to bisect the existing diameters (find the diameter exactly in the middle).

Ask students to measure the diameter of the circle and find the following ratios: (1) the perimeter of the hexagon to the diameter of the circle and (2) the perimeter of the dodecagon to the diameter of the circle. Ask students to compare the ratios in light of what they know about pi. This is the first technique used to estimate pi—increasing the number of sides in a polygon inscribed in a circle. Remind students how tedious this would be using fractions and having no calculators.

For the second part of this investigation, reread page 16, which describes the method used by Bryson, which was to inscribe and circumscribe a polygon and then average the two perimeters. Explain to students they are going to explore this technique using the second circle (Circle B) on their record sheet. Students can use their data from the first circle for the inscribed hexagon, as the circles are the same size.

Illustrate how to circumscribe a hexagon around a circle. Here are two techniques. The first is to draw a line segment outside of a circle that touches it in only one place:

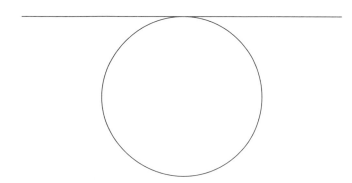

Then, using a protractor or angle ruler, draw the next line segment by forming a 120-degree interior angle with the existing line, being sure the new line touches the circle in just one spot:

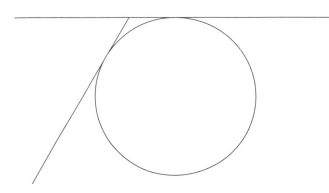

Continue this until the hexagon is complete. Note that accurate measuring is essential for this construction and students may need to adjust if they are not measuring very carefully. To check their accuracy, tell students that if they draw a diameter through one vertex of the hexagon and extend it beyond the circle in both directions, it should pass through the opposite vertex. Some students may realize that once they have drawn a few sides, they have figured out the length of one segment of the hexagon and therefore can calculate the perimeter without drawing all the sides. This is good thinking (if they can justify that the side they have drawn is accurate)!

A second technique uses diameters, as with the inscribed hexagon, and some estimation.

1. Draw a diameter, but extend it about an inch outside of the circle on both sides.

2. Repeat the process, with the new diameter forming a 60-degree angle in the center of the circle with the first diameter.

3. Repeat this process a third time. These lines lead out to where the vertices of the hexagon will be placed.

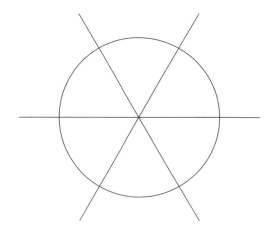

4. Students must figure out the where the vertices of the hexagon go on the extended three diameters (or six radii). The easiest way to

do this is by estimation. Ask students to draw a line segment connecting two of the extended radii, such that (1) the segment touches the circle in one spot, exactly in the middle of the two segments, and (2) the length of each extended radii (from the center of the circle to a vertex of the hexagon) is the same. Ask students to check using their ruler.

5. Once the first segment is drawn accurately, the others come more easily. Students can continue to use the same technique as for the first segment. Or, since the interior angle of a hexagon is 120 degrees, they can use their angle ruler or protractor and the existing segment to create the next new segment.

Ask students to average the perimeters of the inscribed and circumscribed hexagons and to look at the ratio of the average perimeter to the diameter of the circle.

Note: Inscribing and circumscribing circles can be done using technology, such as GeoGebra or Geometer's Sketchpad. GeoGebra is free—go to www.geogebra.org/cms. To use it, the computer must have Java, which is also free. Use of technology can affect the focus of the lesson. It will speed up the process greatly, allowing more time for exploring more circles. Doing the activity by hand offers important lessons in measuring angles and doing constructions, and is more like the way pi was estimated historically.

Invite students to share the advantages and disadvantages of the two different strategies for finding pi (making polygons of more and more sides versus inscribing and circumscribing hexagons).

Ask students if the ratio of the hexagons to the diameter (the approximation of pi) would change if the size of the circle changed. Once they have made predictions, ask them to investigate this, using Circles C and D. If you want students to explore more different-sized circles, distribute the additional circles provided in the Blackline Masters or have students create their own. Let students know that they can use either strategy to investigate the other circles.

At the end of the lesson, invite students to report their findings. Record each student's ratio of perimeter to diameter on the board or an overhead transparency, keeping one list for the first technique and a separate list for the second technique. Again, ask students which technique they think is more accurate or preferable.

Return to Archimedes and ask what his work would have been like, given that he had no technology, no zero, and no decimal point. Conclude the lesson by asking students to write a summary of what strategy they think was the most effective in approximating pi and why.

Leonardo's Horse

Did you know that an unfinished project of Leonardo da Vinci's was completed just recently—in 1999—by an American named Nina Akamu? *Leonardo's Horse*, by Jean Fritz (2001), tells the story of Leonardo's dream to create a bronze horse. He worked on diagramming it for years and created a 24-foot clay model in 1493, but when he died in 1519, he still had not created the bronze horse. The Akamu sculpture is now sitting in the town in Italy where da Vinci's bronze statue would have been.

In creating the statue, Nina Akamu first built an 8-foot model, then finally the 24-foot statue. This fact offers the opportunity to explore the rate of growth for volume. Students might think that the second model was three times the size of the first, but this is not so. When dimensions are tripled in each direction, area is increased ninefold, and the volume is increased twenty-seven times. In this lesson, which includes concepts in geometry, algebra, and measurement, students build "statues" with multilink cubes to explore this growth phenomenon.

MATERIALS

Leonardo's Horse record sheets, 1 per student (see Blackline Masters)

multilink or interlocking cubes, about 300 per small group of students

centimeter grid paper, 1 sheet per student (see Blackline Masters), or graphing calculators, 1 per student

The Investigation

Begin this lesson by asking students what they know of Leonardo da Vinci. Students are likely to know that he was a famous artist, but not necessarily know what works are his most famous. Ask students if they know anything about da Vinci's horse as you show them the cover of the book.

Read the book to the class. It is long enough that it might be necessary to read some passages and save other passages for independent reading. When you have finished the book, ask students why sculptors build a small model before creating the large one. Explain to students that they are going to build their own simple model and see what will happen to the measurements when the dimensions are enlarged by a factor of eight. Distribute the record sheets and ask students to predict what will happen to a statue's length, base area, surface area, and volume when its height is increased eight times.

Once students have recorded their predictions, pass out the interlocking cubes and direct groups to build a 2-by-2-by-2 cube as their model for a large cubic statue. Next, ask students to record the data about their model's base area, surface area, and volume on the table provided on the record sheet. Once they have this first model built and the measurements recorded, ask students to build a 3-by-3-by-3 cube and find and record its base area, surface area, and volume. Direct students to continue this procedure for a 4-by-4-by-4 cube and a 5-by-5-by-5 cube. Ask students to work collaboratively in their groups to build each of the new models and to help each other with the measurements. Each student in the group can build a different model to be more efficient.

Once they have completed the table up through the 5-by-5-by-5 cube, tell students to find patterns in the table. Ask them to use these patterns to figure out each measurement for a 6-by-6-by-6 cube, without building it, then a 7-by-7-by-7 cube and an 8-by-8-by-8 one. Ask students to explore their table again, looking at the changes when each of the model's side lengths is increased by 1. After students have had some time to find patterns, call the class together to share the findings.

The classroom discussion should first focus on the relationships or rules across the table. In other words, if you know the side length, how could you determine the other measurements? The length grows in a linear fashion, but the area grows in a quadratic fashion (l^2), and the volume grows in a cubic fashion (l^3). Students are likely to describe these patterns in words.

Next students can address the issue related to the story: What happens when the length is increased by eight? Leading into this discussion, you might ask:

- What happens to the area of the base when the side length is doubled?

- What happens to the other measurements (surface area and volume) when the length is doubled?

- What happens to the other measurements if the length is quadrupled?

After students have completed the table, ask them to create graphs of their data on grid paper or with a graphing calculator, with length of the base serving as the independent variable. This means they will be graphing (x_1, y_1) = (length of side, area of base), (x_2, y_2) = (length of side, surface area), and (x_3, y_3) = (length of side, volume).

After students have finished their tables and graphs, ask them to discuss in their groups what patterns they notice about the rate of growth. Challenge them to create equations to describe each of the relationships. Then have them complete the final item on the record sheet, explaining their findings to future sculptors.

The Librarian Who Measured the Earth

The Librarian Who Measured the Earth, by Kathryn Lasky (1994), a biography about Eratosthenes, offers interesting highlights of his life, focusing on how he questioned and eventually found the measurement for the circumference of the earth. Eratosthenes became the librarian in Alexandria, Egypt, at a time when Alexandria was the home of scholars. With access to all the records in the library and to other scholars, Eratosthenes was able to explore and solve numerous problems in many areas, including geography and mathematics. This beautifully illustrated book emphasizes that Eratosthenes was a questioner and a problem solver.

The mathematics that Eratosthenes used can prompt a powerful investigation into circles and triangles. In this lesson, students examine the relationship between central angles of a circle and its circumference. Students measure the central angle and the arc length it creates and then estimate the circumference of the circle using that information.

MATERIALS

spherical object such as a basketball or a beach ball

cardboard circles of various sizes, 1 per small group of students

pieces of string, about 1 foot long, 1 per small group of students

protractors or angle rulers, 1 per small group of students

rulers marked in centimeters and millimeters, 1 per small group of students

The Librarian Who Measured the Earth **record sheets,** 1 per small group of students (see Blackline Masters)

calculators, 1 per student

The Investigation

To introduce this lesson, hold up the ball and ask students how they might determine its circumference. It is likely that they will suggest wrapping a tape measure or string around the ball at its widest place. Ask students if they can imagine ways to measure a really large sphere; ask if they have ideas about how the earth and other planets were measured. Read the book to the class. If time is limited, start with the passage on page 30, where the detailed discussion of the earth's circumference begins.

After finishing the book, ask students, "Do you think that you can use Eratosthenes's approach to find the circumference of different-sized circles?" Place students in groups. Give each group one cardboard circle, a piece of string, a protractor or angle ruler, a ruler, a pair of scissors, and a record sheet. Also make sure that each student has a calculator. Then ask each group to name and secretly measure the circumference of its circle, as carefully as possible. Depending on the experience of the students, they can determine circumference by direct measurement or by measuring the diameter or radius and using the formula. Ask each group to find the center of its circle and, using the protractor (or angle ruler), create a sector with an angle measure between 5 degrees and 45 degrees, cut it out, and name it, so later on the students will know it is their section.

When groups are ready, have each group pass its sector to another group. Tell the groups to determine the circumference, to the nearest hundredth of a centimeter, of the circle the sector belongs to. They can do this by reversing the process they used to create their sectors. They must determine the arc length and the angle measure of the sector (see table on record sheet). Have students repeat this process two or three more times, passing on the section they have for a new section from another group. With each new sector, ask students to rotate their jobs—who measures the angle, who measures the arc, who determines the circumference, and who records the data in the table.

As the groups are working, prepare a list of the names of the circles with the actual circumference measurement for each as determined by the group that started with that circle. Once all groups have worked with four circles, ask them to predict how accurate they think their work is. Questions might include:

- How accurate do you think your circumferences are? (for example, within how many centimeters or millimeters?)

- Do you think that smaller circles will have more, less, or the same error of measurement that bigger circles have?

- If a circle measured 20 centimeters around, but you approximated it to be 19 centimeters, what would be the percent of error? ($\frac{1}{20} = 5$ percent error)

Post the actual measurements for the circumferences of the circles. Ask students to find the percent of error in their work. After students have done this, ask them what could have caused the errors. Students might suggest cutting errors, measurement errors by the original measurers or their group, and rounding errors. Return to the story, reminding students of how Eratosthenes measured the arc length. Ask students to determine his percent of error in his measurement (see page 44 of the book for the values needed).

The Man Who Made Parks

The Story of Parkbuilder Frederick Law Olmsted

The Man Who Made Parks, by Frieda Wishinsky (1999), explains that after trying out many professions without finding happiness, Olmsted got the idea to build a park for the city of New York. He became the park superintendent and was therefore in charge of preparing 840 acres of the polluted and disgusting land that had been set aside for this purpose. When the land was cleared, a park design was needed. A competition was held to determine the designer. Olmsted and his architect friend Calvert Vaux won.

This lesson, which focuses on number and operations, incorporates a similar "competition" for a park design. It involves two activities; use either one or both. First, students explore square numbers and square roots by considering the dimensions of different-sized square parks and their areas. Second, students find fractional parts of a rectangular region (park), then solve fraction puzzles about the size of different regions in a park. Moving between the actual size and its fractional representation of the whole strengthens students' understanding of the relative size of fractions and helps build their proportional reasoning skills.

MATERIALS

centimeter grid paper, 2–3 sheets per student (see Blackline Masters)

overhead transparency or piece of chart paper

optional: calculators, 1 per pair of students

Activity 1: Estimating Square Parks

After reading *The Man Who Made Parks*, tell students that they are going to engage in a park design competition. First, they must consider the dimensions of the park. Ask students what is meant by *dimensions*. After they suggest the dimensions of the park are the length and the width, ask them what is true about the dimensions if the park is a square. Explain that they are going to explore the side lengths of square parks of various sizes.

Give one sheet of the grid paper to each student. Ask students to outline on the grid paper a square park that is 25 square units. Have them compare their drawing with a partner or small group and discuss any differences. Confirm that the side length is 5 units. Next, ask students to outline a square park that is 16 square units. Again, have them compare their drawing with a partner or small group, discuss any differences, and confirm that the side length is 4 units. Continue with more examples such as a square park with an area of 64 square units and one with 100 square units.

Now, ask students to determine the dimensions of a square park with an area of 36 square units *without drawing it* and to explain their thinking. Discuss with the students the patterns they see when they multiply the length by the width. Ask students for the area of a square park that hasn't been mentioned and that would be simple to outline on grid paper.

On the board, list the numbers that were used for the park areas the class has discussed so far. Tell the students that these numbers are perfect square numbers because they are the result of a whole number multiplied by itself, such as 5×5 or 6×6. Elicit other square numbers not in the list and add them to the list as students suggest them.

Give students a square number from the list and tell them that it is the area of a square park. Have them tell you the side length of the square. Ask students if they know what these numbers are called. A side length of a square is the *square root* of the area of the square. For example, the square root of 16 is 4 because 4 times 4 is 16. Practice this with square numbers from 1 to 100 (1, 4, 9, 16, 25, 36, 49, 64, 81, 100).

Next, have students estimate the square root of numbers that are not perfect squares. For example, ask, "If I had ten square units for a square park, about how long would the side lengths be?" Students might use the following reasoning to determine the approximate length:

If the park were nine square units, the side lengths would be three. Because the park is a little bigger than nine square units, the side lengths would be more than three. However, ten is less than the perfect square number sixteen, so the side lengths would be less than four. Ten is closer to nine than it is to sixteen, so the square root would be closer to three.

Ask students how they might test their estimates, and allow time for them to do so. Alternatively, have students multiply 3.1 by 3.1 and see if the result is close to 10. If possible, have them check their guesses using the square root function on a calculator. The idea behind estimating is that they can make reasonable guesses based on what they already know. The calculator is not essential, but it does help students to quickly see if an estimate is reasonable.

Have students continue to estimate square roots of numbers that are not perfect squares by using perfect square numbers and their roots as guides. Following are several examples:

- What are the dimensions of a square park with an area of 50 square units? Or, what is the square root of fifty?

- What is the square root of eighteen?

- What is the square root of thirty?

- What is the square root of seventy-six?

- What is the square root of ninety-five?

The New York City park, eventually renamed Central Park, enclosed 840 acres, which is 43,560 square feet. Have students approximate the dimensions of that park if it were a square.

Activity 2: Designing a Park

As an additional or alternative investigation, have students consider other ways to enclose 43,560 square feet, such as a nonsquare rectangle or even as a composite of rectangles.

Tell students that, like in the book, they are each going to design their own park. Put the following guidelines on a transparency or chart paper and display for the class.

You have 100 square acres. You want 36 acres to be paths for walking, jogging, or bike riding. You want the remaining acres to be used as follows:

- $\frac{1}{2}$ *to be fields for ball playing, kite flying, and so on*
- $\frac{1}{4}$ *to be wooded and remain "rugged"*
- $\frac{1}{8}$ *to be gardens*
- $\frac{1}{16}$ *to be a large pond for ice-skating in the winter and fishing in the summer*
- $\frac{1}{16}$ *to be for playgrounds*

Distribute grid paper. Instruct students to follow the guidelines and to make a key for their design, indicating with color coding or symbols what each section represents. The areas for each feature do not necessarily have to be together.

Have students post their work when completed. Discuss as a class how many squares they used for the paths (36), fields (32), woods (16), gardens (8), pond (4), and playgrounds (4). Discuss how they came up with these numbers and how they developed their designs.

Here are two additional opportunities, in a puzzle format, for students to work with fractions as they did in designing their parks.

In a park, a landscaper planted red, pink, and white rose bushes. One-fourth of the rose bushes were white, one-fourth were pink, and one-half were red. There were six white rose bushes. Answer the following questions and include pictures in your work.

- *How many rose bushes were pink?*
- *How many rose bushes were red?*
- *How many rose bushes in all?*

Thirty acres of a park were used for ball fields. Two-fifths of the space was used for several baseball fields and several softball diamonds. One-fifth was used for a couple of soccer fields, and the remaining two-fifths was left open for "free play" fields. Answer the following questions and explain your thinking.

- *How many acres were used for the baseball and softball fields?*
- *How many acres were used for the soccer fields?*
- *How many acres were used for the free play fields?*

Once students have solved these fraction puzzles, have them create their own.

Made You Look

How Advertising Works and Why You Should Know

An interesting chapter book written for teens, *Made You Look,* by Shari Graydon (2003), presents the history of advertising, advertising strategies, why advertisers target kids, and how advertising can be disguised. Throughout the book are text boxes labeled "Don't Try This at Home!" that offer topics for the reader to investigate. As with many nonfiction works, this book contains important and relevant knowledge that can help adolescents navigate their world.

Inspired by the chapter titled "And Now, a Newer, Happier You!" this data analysis lesson is designed to increase students' awareness of the extent and nature of advertising. Students work in pairs to select a teen magazine from home or the library, determine what percent of the total issue is advertising, and prepare a report on the types and frequency of advertisements that they find.

MATERIALS

teen or youth magazines, at least 1 per pair of students

sticky notes, 1 per student

Made You Look **record sheets,** 1 per pair of students (see Blackline Masters)

optional: computer with spreadsheet software

The Investigation

Prior to this lesson, ask students to bring a favorite magazine to class or allow time for them to get one from the library. Have them use their own magazines or work together on the same one.

To launch this lesson, ask students to record on a sticky note a favorite commercial or advertisement and bring their sticky to the board. Ask students what features these advertisements have in common and how they differ. If time allows, sort advertisements by common feature, such as *humor* or *convincing data.* Explain that a lot of research goes into creating advertisements, most importantly, finding out what will be liked by the intended audience.

Share the title of the book and read any sections that will interest your students. Read all or part of the chapter "And Now, a Newer, Happier You!" which begins on page 33. After reading, ask students to estimate how much of a typical teen magazine might be devoted to advertisements. Ask what strategies advertisers might use to target young people and teens. Students may brainstorm approaches such as "this is cool or popular," "everyone uses/has this," "research shows . . . ," "some famous person has this; so should you . . . ," "boys will like you if you have this," and so on. If they do not have these ideas, ask them to review the advertisements in their magazines and find a strategy for one or two. You can also show particular advertisements and ask students to characterize the strategies they use.

Once students have an idea of how to characterize advertisements, ask them to work with a partner and go through their magazine two times. The first time, they are to calculate the percent of pages that have advertisements, rounding to the nearest fourth of a page. In some cases, they will have to judge whether the page is an advertisement or an article. Set a time limit for this review, as students can get bogged down looking at the magazine.

The second time they review the magazine, they are to study each advertisement, characterize it or give it a type, record that type in the table on their record sheet, and mark a tally. When they come to a second advertisement that they believe is the same type, they simply need to add a tally to the same row of the table. By the end of the second review, they should have three to ten types of ads and tallies for each.

Ask pairs to prepare a presentation that tells what they found in their magazines and includes a graph. Depending on your curriculum goals, ask students to specifically create a pie graph or a frequency chart, or both, or ask students to select a display that best illustrates what they found. Students can use a spreadsheet program or create graphs by hand. Ask students to share their results with the class. In conclusion, ask students what they have learned about advertising and what surprised them. If time permits, share some passages from Chapter 6, which addresses the impact of advertising on young people.

Mathematical Scandals

Mathematical Scandals, by Theoni Pappas (1997), contains more than twenty intriguing, if not scandalous, historical events related to mathematics. One is the cover-up of the discovery of irrational numbers. The Pythagoreans could not accept that there was a need for any kind of number other than whole numbers. When Hippasus publicly shared that the diagonal of a unit square was $\sqrt{2}$, he was expelled from the society of the Pythagoreans. Some accounts actually state that he was put to death. Not long after Hippasus, Theodorus used the notion of $\sqrt{2}$ to create the wheel of Theodorus. ("Irrational Numbers Can 'In-Spiral' You" [Lewis 2007] is a wonderful reference for further reading about the wheel of Theodorus.)

In this geometry lesson, students explore the Pythagorean theorem, in particular, the wheel of Theodorus. The wheel is constructed by creating right triangles such that the hypotenuse of one triangle becomes one side of the next triangle, with the other side measuring 1 centimeter. The first triangle has sides measuring 1 cm, and therefore, its hypotenuse is $\sqrt{2}$ cm. The next triangle has sides of $\sqrt{2}$ cm and 1 cm, and therefore, its hypotenuse is $\sqrt{3}$ cm. The next has sides of $\sqrt{3}$ cm and 1 cm and a hypotenuse of $\sqrt{4}$ cm or 2 cm, and so on.

MATERIALS

centimeter dot paper, 1 sheet per student (see Blackline Masters)

metric rulers, 1 per student

calculators, 1 per student

12-by-18-inch construction paper, 1 sheet per student

The Investigation

Ask students if they know anything about the Pythagoreans. Explain that they were members of a secret math society with strict rules and were not individuals that you would want to cross. Read "The Irrational Number Cover-Up" (1–6) to the class. Students may have a hard time believing that a math club could be so elite—and dangerous! Explain to students that they are going to look at the proof that Hippasus bravely presented to the world.

Hand out one sheet of dot paper and a ruler to each student. Ask students to create a right triangle with legs that each measure 1 centimeter. Ask them how long the hypotenuse of that triangle is. Students usually think that it is 1 centimeter and are surprised to learn it is not. Using the Pythagorean theorem, have students find the hypotenuse, which is actually $\sqrt{2}$ cm. Then ask students to measure the hypotenuse so that they can see it is about 1.4 cm. Using calculators, they can estimate $\sqrt{2}$ at 1.4142.

Ask students to start in a new spot on their dot paper and make a right triangle with legs that each measure 2 centimeters. The hypotenuse of this triangle connects three dots. Ask students how long the hypotenuse is. Using the Pythagorean theorem, they will find that it is $\sqrt{8}$ cm. Again, ask students to measure the hypotenuse. Some students may notice that they can just double their measurement from the previous triangle and get 2.8 centimeters. Again, they can check the approximation of $\sqrt{8}$ on their calculators. If needed, students can also explore this phenomenon with isosceles right triangles that have legs that each measure 3 centimeters.

Ask students, "How are you going to draw a triangle that has a hypotenuse of the square root of three centimeters? In other words, how can you get a triangle that would be bigger than the triangle with sides of one centimeter and smaller than the triangle with sides of two centimeters?" Students may suggest a triangle with sides of 1 centimeter and 2 centimeters, but this leads to a hypotenuse of $\sqrt{5}$ cm.

Ask students to turn their dot paper over to the blank side. Explain to them that they are going to apply the ideas of Hippasus (b. 500 BC) in the same way that Theodorus (465–398 BC) did, creating what is now known as the wheel of Theodorus. Give the following instructions, making sure all students have completed step 1 before explaining step 2. Model each step on the overhead.

1. Use a ruler and start in the center of your paper. Draw a right triangle with 1-centimeter legs by measuring the length of each side and making sure the angle is exactly 90°.

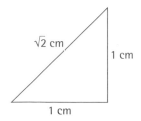

2. Use the hypotenuse of the triangle you just drew as a side of a new triangle. Draw another side, 1 centimeter long, perpendicular to the $\sqrt{2}$ cm side. Draw the new hypotenuse.

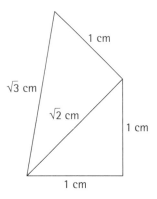

Figure 25–1: A student-created wheel of Theodorus (reduced in size).

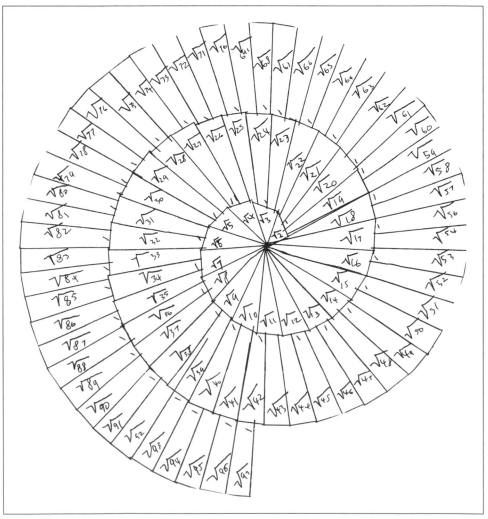

3. Using the Pythagorean theorem, check that the new hypotenuse is √3 cm.

4. Repeat this process again. The next triangle will have a side of √3 cm, a new side of 1 centimeter, and a hypotenuse that measures √4 cm, or 2 cm.

It is important to make sure students are measuring both the 90-degree angles, using a corner of a piece of paper, and the 1-centimeter sides very carefully. If students have successfully created three complete triangles, they are ready to build their wheel of Theodorus.

Distribute one sheet of construction paper to each student. Ask students to start in the center of the paper and to measure very accurately. Ask students to use the same process of constructing triangles to make the wheel out to √30 cm. At that point, they'll see the wheel begin to form. Students can complete this task for homework. Some students have become so involved in creating their wheels that they have continued until they ran out of paper—reading over √350 cm! (See Figures 25–1 and 25–2.)

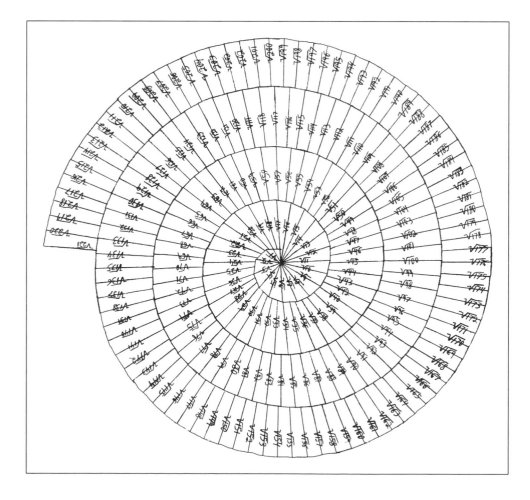

Figure 25–2: Another student-created wheel of Theodorus (reduced in size).

The Mathematical Universe

An Alphabetical Journey Through the Great Proofs, Problems, and Personalities

The Mathematical Universe, by William Dunham (1994), is full of fascinating stories about mathematics, mathematicians, and historical events. While some of the 320 pages of content may be beyond middle school students, much of it discusses historical topics and mathematics related to young students' lives. For example, on page 106, there is a nice simple proof of why a square encloses more area than a nonsquare rectangle with the same perimeter. The mathematics of this concept is introduced through the legend of Princess Dido, who moved to the northern coast of Africa and was given as much land as she could enclose with the hide of a bull. Princess Dido tore the hide into small strips and enclosed a large semicircle, cleverly gaining more land than had ever been considered possible. It was this land that became the city of Carthage.

This story is considered to be the origin of the mathematical problem of how a fixed perimeter can enclose the biggest area, which is the focus of the geometry and measurement lesson. To explore this problem, students form a string of a given length into different shapes and look for the shape that encloses the largest area. Students are also encouraged to notice relationships between perimeter and area.

MATERIALS

rulers and/or tape measures, 1 per pair or small group of students

pieces of string, slightly longer than 60 centimeters, 1 per pair or small group of students, plus a few extra pieces

princess dido's city record sheets, 1 per pair or small group of students (see Blackline Masters)

large sheets of newsprint, 1 per pair or small group of students

The Investigation

To prepare for this activity, cut pieces of string that are slightly longer than 60 centimeters. You can pick a different size if you wish; however, we selected 60 centimeters because it is a reasonable size for making polygons and allows the side lengths for equilateral triangles and squares to be whole numbers.

To introduce the activity, read aloud the beginning of the chapter titled "Isoperimetric Problem," which is the story of Princess Dido (103–105). Stop at the point where it says she was clever and made long strips; don't read that she made a semicircle yet. Place students in pairs or small groups and ask them to share what they think Princess Dido is going to do. After a few minutes, distribute the rulers and string and tell students to tie the ends so that they can't pull apart and the string measures 60 centimeters after it is tied. Explain that this is going to represent the perimeter Princess Dido made from her bull hide strips. Explain that she wants to make a shape that will get her as much land as possible. Have students record different shapes and the areas that can be enclosed by the string on their record sheets. Encourage students to consider all types of shapes. Once students have tried four shapes and measured their areas, ask different groups to share what they think would be the best shape for the princess's plot. Allow groups to debate with each other about the solution that maximizes area.

After this sharing, explain to students that Princess Dido realized that she could use the coast (considering it a straight line) as one of her borders. Ask students to untie their string (or replace the string) and to investigate the problem again, knowing they have one side for "free," which won't use any of the 60 centimeters. Have groups prepare their solution on large newsprint or a transparency. When everyone is ready, have the students share their results.

When all groups have shared, read the remainder of the chapter. It explains the idea of isoperimetric (same perimeter) in a way that integrates mathematics with history.

In conclusion, ask students to consider what they would do if they had 60 yards of fencing and wanted to enclose a space for their pet. Ask them to write an argument that states what shapes would be best to use and what shapes would be worst to use and why.

Numbers

Facts, Figures and Fiction

Numbers: Facts, Figures and Fiction, by Richard Phillips (2004), is about numbers, particularly the counting numbers from 0 to 156, including a description of the special characteristics for each number. The numbers from 157 to 1,000 are mentioned more briefly, including some interesting facts about some very large numbers. Fun facts include cultural connections, tantalizing problems, and anecdotes, all of which provide many opportunities to engage in mathematics.

Because the focus of this book is on whole numbers and their characteristics, it is a perfect match to number theory: factors, multiples, perfect squares, and so on. In this lesson, students select their favorite number and describe it to an audience using the writing style of a feature article. This lesson can be used as an assessment for a unit on number theory. It can also be a collaborative project with an English teacher.

MATERIALS

guidelines for favorite number report, copy per student (see Blackline Masters)

computers with Internet access for reference and for composing

calculators, 1 per student

The Investigation

Begin the lesson by asking students to name a number, any number, that they think is *not* interesting. Suppose someone calls out, "Twenty-nine." Ask if that happens to be someone's favorite number. If it is, then ask the class to pick a different uninteresting number. Once the class has settled on a number that no one finds interesting, read about that number in *Numbers: Facts, Figures and Fiction*. Now ask the class for another uninteresting number and read about it. Do this several times.

Explain to students that today they are going to be investigative reporters, gathering facts, figures, and fiction about a favorite number. In setting up this task, ask students to review the number theory topics that need to be included in their work. These might include all or some of the following:

- prime and composite numbers

- factors

- multiples

- prime factorization

- squares

Then, put on a journalist's hat and discuss aspects of good writing, including the following:

- audience (readers of a newspaper, not students in this class)

- purpose (to show the specialness of the number by describing in detail its characteristics and other facts about it)

- style (what might go in an introduction, body, and conclusion)

- visual supports (what might accompany the text to illustrate the ideas)

Ask students to pick a number from one to one hundred and write it on a sheet of paper. Then give each student a copy of the guidelines for the favorite number report and tell them to complete Part A. This will provide the skeleton for their feature article. Once students have drafted their ideas, allow them to go to the computers to do research and writing. Students can research their number using the websites listed on the guidelines handout or any others they are able to find. If there are not enough computers for everyone, pair students and allow fifteen minutes for each pair to search for interesting facts about one number and then switch and search for information about the other number, or have pairs work on one number they both like and do the whole project together.

Once students have their facts, tell them to write their feature article, including visuals and interesting facts. Remind them to explain why they chose the number.

If time allows, pair students so they can edit each other's work. Explain that as editors, they need to check that the math facts are correct and that the writing is interesting, and then give feedback to the author.

When everyone is ready, have a few volunteers read their articles to the class. Challenge the students to listen for mathematical errors, to provide additional facts about the number, and to find commonalities with their own number. If you prefer, collect and review the articles, then provide time for another revision session and, finally, a sharing session.

The Popcorn Book

In *The Popcorn Book,* by Tomie de Paola (1978), twins are making popcorn. As one explains what he is doing to make the popcorn, the other is reading interesting historical facts about popcorn. It is fun to have two people read this book and/or act it out.

In the story, too much unpopped corn is placed in the pan, and it produces a room full of popcorn. Students investigate the relationship between unpopped and popped popcorn in terms of volume and create an algebraic expression to describe it.

Also in the story is this statistic: In the United States, 500,000,000 pounds of popcorn are popped every year. Students work in groups to determine what this amount of corn kernels might look like.

MATERIALS: ACTIVITY 1

zip-top plastic bags with varying amounts of popcorn kernels, ranging from $\frac{1}{8}$ to $\frac{1}{2}$ cup, 1 per small group of students

measuring cups, 1 per small group of students

popcorn poppers, 1 or 2

large bowl, 1 per group

optional: grid paper

MATERIALS: ACTIVITY 2

zip-top plastic bags of approximately 2 cups of popcorn kernels, 1 per small group of students

kitchen scale

measuring cups, 1 per small group of students

small boxes (shoe box size or smaller; sizes can vary), 1 per small group of students

Activity 1: How Much Popcorn?

Read the story, or if possible, have two students read the story to the class. After reading the entire story, ask students what they learned about popcorn that they didn't already know. Ask students to predict what ratio exists between the volume of unpopped and popped popcorn. Ask students how they can use algebraic reasoning to solve this problem and what data they might gather to figure out the answer to this question. Create a class table on the board with three columns. Label the columns *Unpopped Volume*, *Popped Volume*, and *Unpopped/Popped*, respectively. Direct each group to do the following:

1. Select a bag of unpopped popcorn.

2. Measure the amount of popcorn in the bag using a measuring cup.

3. Pop the popcorn.

4. Measure it again using the measuring cup.

5. Record the information in the class table.

Ask students to find the ratio between the two measurements and put their data on the class table. Once the table is completed, have students compute the average of the ratios. This data can be graphed, with the unpopped corn on the *x*-axis and the popped corn on the *y*-axis (or vice versa). This ratio represents the rate of change, the slope, or the proportional relationship between the two quantities. These concepts are interrelated and central to understanding algebra. Ask students to use the data in the table and/or the graph to create two equations, one that can be used to find the volume of popped corn if they know the volume of the unpopped corn, and one that can be used to determine the amount of unpopped corn if they know the amount of popped corn. Ask students to use their formulas to determine the volume of popcorn that might be produced if 2 cups of unpopped corn were put into the pan (as it appears is done in the story). Ask students to figure out if they wanted 5 gallons of popcorn for a school event, how much unpopped corn they would need. Remind the class that there are 16 cups in 1 gallon.

Summarize the lesson by pointing out that algebraic formulas, like the ones they used to relate unpopped to popped corn, can be used to predict and plan, for example, in this case, how much popcorn to buy for a party. Explain that this is called *mathematical modeling*.

Activity 2: Half Billion Pounds of Popcorn

This investigation can be done following Activity 1 or on its own. Write *500,000,000* on the board. Ask students what that number is. Ask: "How many millions is it? How many billions is it? How many one-hundred-fifty-pound people might it take to equal five hundred million pounds?"

Ask students to work in groups to brainstorm how they might figure out and illustrate what a half billion pounds of unpopped popcorn would look like, that is, how much space it would occupy. After a few minutes, ask each group to share its ideas with the class. Students should come up with a strategy that includes weighing a particular amount of popcorn kernels and finding how much space it occupies by filling a container. Distribute the bags of popcorn kernels, the measuring cups, and the boxes. Note that each group will not have enough popcorn to fill the box, but students can estimate what fraction of the box is filled and determine the weight of a full box.

Have students use the strategy they selected and prepare a report that tells what 500,000,000 pounds of popcorn kernels might look like. Explanations of how much space the unpopped corn would take up should be compared to the size of familiar objects, such as a classroom, a football field, or a swimming pool.

If students have completed the first activity, ask them to determine the volume of *popped* popcorn consumed in one year in the United States, using the formulas they came up with in Activity 1.

What Happened to the Mammoths?

And Other Explorations of Science in Action

> *What Happened to the Mammoths?* by Jack Myers (2000), includes twelve interesting animal mysteries that bring science and math to life by making them much more than just a collection of data and facts.
>
> The purpose of this lesson is to provide students with data and have them analyze them and draw conclusions. To do so requires giving students the chart from this story, asking them to analyze it, and then reading the story as a culmination, rather than an introduction, to the lesson. The focus of this lesson is on ratio and proportional reasoning.

MATERIALS

What Happened to the Mammoths? **record sheet,** 1 per student (see Blackline Masters)

optional: calculators, 1 per student

The Investigation

To launch the lesson, tell students that they are going to investigate a surprising thing about alligators. Ask them to imagine that they are alligator experts and someone has approached them with some data and asked them what they think the data mean. Give each student a record sheet, which includes the following chart:

Temperature (Celsius)	26°	28°	30°	32°	34°	36°
Number of Eggs	50	100	100	100	100	50
Number of Females Born	10	96	97	85	0	0
Number of Males Born	0	0	0	13	94	7
Number of Eggs That Died	40	4	3	2	6	43

Ask the students to study the data on the recording sheet and record on notebook paper what they notice. Students should conclude that the best temperature for hatching alligator eggs is between 28 and 34 degrees Celsius. They should also notice that at cooler temperatures the eggs that hatched were all female and at the higher temperatures, the eggs that hatched were all male. Help students conclude that this is evidence that the temperature of the nest affects whether a newborn alligator is male or female, which is quite different than how gender is determined for the offspring of mammals!

Ask students to write a ratio of males born to females born for each temperature as well as for all the alligators in the experiment. They should find them to be the following:

Temperature	Ratio of Males Born to Females Born
26°	0:10
28°	0:96
30°	0:97
32°	13:85
34°	94:0
36°	7:0
Total	114:288

Ask students, "What is the ratio of males to females in humans?" They should estimate the ratio to be about 1:1 because there is approximately a 50 percent chance that a baby will be male and a 50 percent chance that it will be female. This is a great opportunity to discuss *part-to-part* ratios and *part-to-whole* ratios. Ask students which they are using here. They should be able to identify it as a part-to-part ratio because they are comparing the number of males with the number of females. Ask students how to change these ratios into part-to-whole ratios. Volunteers will most likely suggest that they would need to know the total number of alligators that were born, which they could get by adding the number of males and females together. They would then be able to conclude that the ratio of males to alligators is 114:402 and the ratio of females to alligators is 288:402.

Ask students, "When you look at the data, how do you think the ratio of males to females for wild alligators compares with the ratio of males to females for humans?" Following this discussion, read pages 22 through 26, with the exception of the blue box "Temperature and Dinosaur Eggs" on the last page. Save this for the end of the lesson. Ask the students how their conclusions based on the data they analyzed compare with the data the scientists described in what you just read to them.

In a four-year study of alligator eggs that were incubated in the wild, the ratio of hatched males to females was found to be 1:5. To continue working with ratios, instruct students to find approximately how many alligators were male and how many were female out of the 8,000 eggs that were collected for this experiment. They should conclude that approximately 1,333 were males and 6,665 were females. Have students share their strategies for finding the number of males and females. Some students may use a proportion: $\frac{1}{5} = \frac{x}{8,000 - x}$. Other students may decide to change the ratio into a part-to-whole ratio and find $\frac{1}{6}$ of 8,000 to determine the number of males. Because $\frac{5}{6}$ is female, they would then multiply 1,333 by 5 to get 6,665. Ask students what problems this 1:5 ratio could cause in terms of propagating the species.

Conclude the lesson by reading the information in the blue box titled "Temperature and Dinosaur Eggs" on page 26.

Blackline Masters

Attribute Block Probabilities Record Sheet
Chipping Away at Chocolate Chips Record Sheet
Centimeter Square Dot Paper
Isometric Dot Paper
Everybody Loves Ice Cream Record Sheet
Centimeter Grid Paper
Go Figure! Record Sheet
Instructions for Wreath and Pinwheel Origami
Polygons
G Is for Googol; S Is for Symmetry Record Sheet
If You Hopped Like a Frog Task List
The Motley Fool Investment Guide for Teens Record Sheet
A Negro League Scrapbook Record Sheet
Coordinate Axes Grid Paper
How to Make a (Basic) Origami Bird
Telling Time Record Sheet
Venn Diagram Template
Toy Prices Record Sheet
Inch Grid Paper
Cereal Box Evaluation
If the World Were a Village Topic Cards
Approximating Pi Record Sheet
The Joy of π Additional Circles
Leonardo's Horse Record Sheet
The Librarian Who Measured the Earth Record Sheet
Made You Look Record Sheet
Princess Dido's City Record Sheet
Guidelines for Favorite Number Report
What Happened to the Mammoths? Record Sheet

Attribute Block Probabilities Record Sheet

Use your attribute blocks to find the following probabilities. Record your answers as fractions. You may simplify.

Investigation 1: Red and Thick
$P(\text{red})$
$P(\text{thick})$
$P(\text{red and thick})$

Investigation 2: Thin and Square
$P(\text{thin})$
$P(\text{square})$
$P(\text{thin and square})$

Investigation 3: Create your own
$P(\text{attribute A})$
$P(\text{attribute B})$
$P(\text{attributes A and B})$

Is there a relationship?
Look at the results for each set. What relationship do you see? Record your thinking.

Chipping Away at Chocolate Chips Record Sheet

Part 1: One Minute of Chocolate Chips

It's a fact: 58,000 chocolate chips are made in just one minute! Find out what this looks like by answering the following questions.

1. What could 58,000 chocolate chips surround? Be sure your answer is an object that is familiar to the rest of us. Show your work.

2. What could 58,000 chips cover? Be sure your answer is an object that is familiar to the rest of us. Show your work.

From *Math and Nonfiction, Grades 6–8* by Jennifer M. Bay-Williams and Sherri L. Martinie. © 2009 Math Solutions Publications.

Part 2: More Than One Minute of Chocolate Chips

3. Create a formula to describe the production of chocolate chips.

4. Use your formula to answer the following questions.

   • How many chips are produced in one hour?
   • How long will it take to produce one million chips? One billion chips? One trillion chips? Explain how you figured this out.

5. Using your answers to Questions 1 and 2, what would one billion chips look like? Explain in words, numbers, and/or pictures.

Centimeter Square Dot Paper

From *Math and Nonfiction, Grades 6–8* by Jennifer M. Bay-Williams and Sherri L. Martinie. © 2009 Math Solutions Publications.

Isometric Dot Paper

Everybody Loves Ice Cream Record Sheet

How tall is a stack of 100 ice-cream cones?

1. What is your prediction? _____

2. Complete the table for your stack of cones.

    Kind of cone: _____

Number of Cones	Height of Stack (to the nearest tenth of a cm)
1	
2	
3	
4	
5	
6	
7	
8	
9	
10	
20	
30	
40	
50	

From *Math and Nonfiction, Grades 6–8* by Jennifer M. Bay-Williams and Sherri L. Martinie. © 2009 Math Solutions Publications.

3. If you continue with this pattern, how tall would a stack of 100 cones be? Explain how you determined this.

4. How close was your prediction to the actual height of the stack?

5. Using centimeter grid paper, graph your data.

6. Do your data represent a linear function? Explain why or why not.

7. Write a rule for calculating the height of a stack of any number of cones. How did you come up with your rule?

From *Math and Nonfiction, Grades 6–8* by Jennifer M. Bay-Williams and Sherri L. Martinie. © 2009 Math Solutions Publications.

Centimeter Grid Paper

From *Math and Nonfiction, Grades 6–8* by Jennifer M. Bay-Williams and Sherri L. Martinie. © 2009 Math Solutions Publications.

Go Figure! Record Sheet

Exploring Peas

1. If you cross a white-flowered pea (pp) and a pure purple-flowered pea (PP), what is the probability of getting a white-flowered pea? Explain all possibilities.

2. If you cross two peas that are mixed (Pp), what is the probability of getting a white-flowered pea?

Prediction: _____

Design an experiment to see what actually happens after twenty trials.

Describe Experiment Here	Record Your Data Here

How About Us? Let's Experiment!

3. Can you curl your tongue? Tongue curling is a dominant trait (T). Not being able to curl your tongue is recessive (t).

4. Show the theoretical probability of being a tongue curler if one parent is tt and the other is Tt.

Applying Your Knowledge

5. Under what conditions would the probability of producing a tongue curler be 0? Explain.

6. Under what conditions would the probability of producing a tongue curler be 1? Explain.

From *Math and Nonfiction, Grades 6–8* by Jennifer M. Bay-Williams and Sherri L. Martinie. © 2009 Math Solutions Publications.

7. For each prompt below, write a paragraph related to your genetics exploration.

What we found . . .

What I learned . . .

Instructions for Wreath and Pinwheel Origami

The Wreath

For each square of origami paper, follow these steps:

1. Place the paper with the white side facing up.

2. Fold the square to create four creases through its center: one vertical, one horizontal, and two diagonal. Dashed lines show where the creases should be:

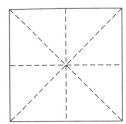

3. Fold the top corners to the center to make the roof of a house.

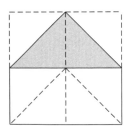

4. Fold the house in half, folding the left side to the right side such that the flaps are on the inside of the fold.

From *Math and Nonfiction, Grades 6–8* by Jennifer M. Bay-Williams and Sherri L. Martinie. © 2009 Math Solutions Publications.

5. Turn the half house sideways and then hold it by the acute angle at the bottom left.

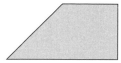

6. Push in the bottom right corner to form a parallelogram.

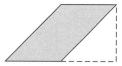

Now follow these steps to put the wreath together:

1. Position one piece with the folded edge to the left and the acute angle at the bottom left.

2. Position the next piece with the folded edge at the top and the acute angle at the upper left.

3. Slide the acute angle on the right piece into the fold pocket of the left piece.

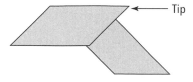

4. Fold down the tips of the left piece into the middle of the right piece.

5. Repeat this process for each piece.

6. Connect the last piece to the first piece.

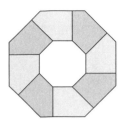

The Pinwheel

Gently slide the sides of the wreath toward the center.

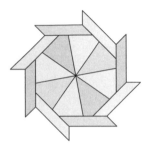

Adapted from *Connected Mathematics: Kaleidoscopes, Hubcaps, and Mirrors*, by G. Lappan, J. T. Fey, W. M. Fitzgerald, S. N. Friel, and E. D. Phillips (La Porte, IN: Prentice Hall/Dale Seymour, 1998), 73–75.

Polygons

G Is for Googol; S Is for Symmetry Record Sheet

1. Sketch the wreath and label all the lines of symmetry.

2. Sketch the wreath again and label all the degrees of rotational symmetry that you see.

3. Sketch the pinwheel and label all the lines of symmetry.

4. Sketch the pinwheel again and label all the degrees of rotational symmetry that you see.

5. Unfold your shape. Use colored pencils to draw all the triangles made by the folds on one piece of paper. Measure and label all the interior angles of each triangle.

6. Describe the types of triangles that you found when you unfolded your shape.

If You Hopped Like a Frog Task List

- A 3-inch frog can jump 60 inches! If you could leap like that, how far would you be able to go in one hop?

- A whooping crane that is 4 feet tall has a 16-inch neck! What fraction of the crane is neck? If you had the same proportions, what size neck would you have?

- Pygmy shrews are tiny land animals with big appetites. A shrew that weighs $\frac{1}{5}$ of an ounce eats about $\frac{3}{5}$ of an ounce of worms and insects each day. How many quarter-pounders would you have to eat to eat like a pygmy shrew?

- A brachiosaurus weighed about 80,000 kilograms! But its brain weighed only 200 grams. If you had the brain of a brachiosaurus, how much would your brain weigh?

- Ants are small and mighty. One ant weighs about $\frac{1}{250}$ of an ounce! It can lift a breadcrumb that weighs about $\frac{1}{5}$ of an ounce. If you were this strong, how much could you lift?

Adapted from *If You Hopped Like a Frog* by David M. Schwartz (New York: Scholastic, 1999).

From *Math and Nonfiction, Grades 6–8* by Jennifer M. Bay-Williams and Sherri L. Martinie. © 2009 Math Solutions Publications.

The Motley Fool Investment Guide for Teens
Record Sheet

A. Complete the tables until your money doubles.

5 Percent Compound Interest

Year	Money Saved	Year	Money Saved
1		9	
2		10	
3		11	
4		12	
5		13	
6		14	
7		15	
8			

11 Percent Compound Interest

Year	Money Saved
1	
2	
3	
4	
5	
6	
7	
8	
9	
10	

13 Percent Compound Interest

Year	Money Saved
1	
2	
3	
4	
5	
6	
7	
8	
9	
10	

B. Graph the money you would have if you start with $100 and earn 10 percent interest over the next twenty years in two-year intervals.

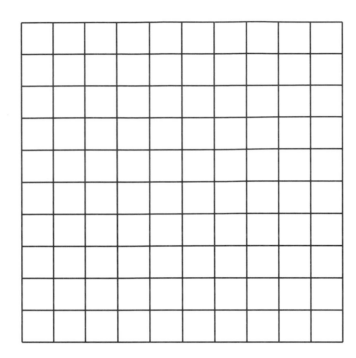

C. Graph the money you would have if you start with $100 and earn exactly $20 in interest each year for twenty years in two-year intervals.

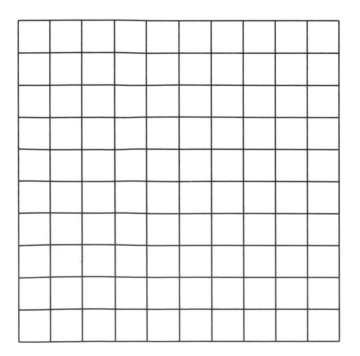

From *Math and Nonfiction, Grades 6–8* by Jennifer M. Bay-Williams and Sherri L. Martinie. © 2009 Math Solutions Publications.

A *Negro League Scrapbook* Record Sheet

1. The table below shows information about five great pitchers. What percent of wins among these greats did Satchel Paige have? What percent of shutouts among these five did he have? What percent of no-hitters?

	Wins	Shutouts	No-Hitters
Roger Clemens	348	46	0
Nolan Ryan	324	61	7
Greg Maddox	335	35	0
Cy Young	511	76	3
Satchel Paige	2,100	300	55

2. What comparisons do you notice between Satchel Paige's pitching statistics and those of other great pitchers? Make three to five mathematical comparisons and list them below:

3. Sports writers like to showcase the skills of great players. Use a separate piece of paper to write a brief sports column about Satchel Paige and his incredible talent. Use percents in your column to compare the pitchers.

Coordinate Axes Grid Paper

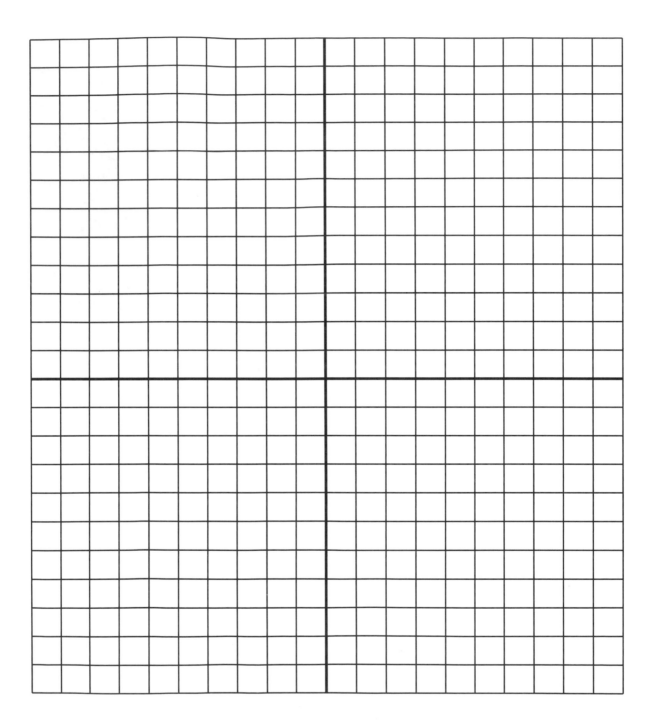

From *Math and Nonfiction, Grades 6–8* by Jennifer M. Bay-Williams and Sherri L. Martinie. © 2009 Math Solutions Publications.

How to Make a (Basic) Origami Bird

1. Place your paper with the colored side facedown. (This will give your bird a white body but colored head, neck, and wings.)

2. Fold your square along a diagonal and then unfold it, leaving it flat. The plain side should still be faceup. Turn the square to a diamond position with the crease line running from top to bottom, then fold the left- and right-side corners in to the center fold and up so the left and right sides meet along the center fold line.

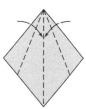

3. At this point the paper should look like an upside-down kite—broad at the bottom and narrowing toward the top.

4. Fold the top corner down to the spot where the left and right corners now meet. This fold makes the bird's neck.

5. Fold the end of that fold back up a little bit. Don't worry about exactly how far you fold it. This smaller fold will be the bird's head.

6. Fold the bird in half away from you (with the colored side facing down) along the crease you made in Step 1. (Make sure all previous folds remain intact.)

7. Pull the neck out from the body so the neck and head are vertical to the body. Make a new crease at the base of the neck.

8. Pull the beak up, and create a new crease on the back of the head.

9. You can pull the wings out at the base to spread out the wings and let the bird sit.

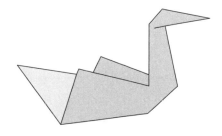

Telling Time Record Sheet

Record the class data from the pendulum experiment in the table below.

String Length	30-Second Swing Rate Trial 1	30-Second Swing Rate Trial 2	30-Second Swing Rate Trial 3	30-Second Swing Rate Average

Graph the class data for string length and average swing rate.

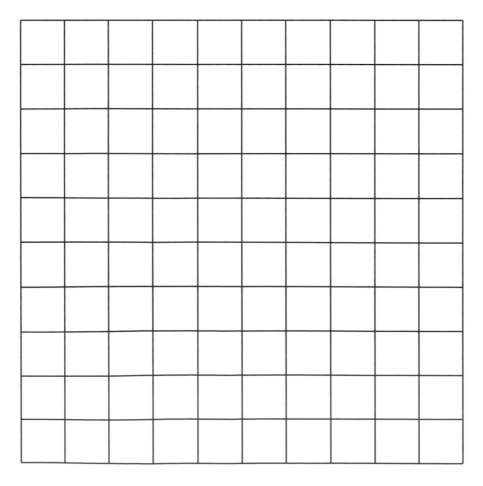

From *Math and Nonfiction, Grades 6–8* by Jennifer M. Bay-Williams and Sherri L. Martinie. © 2009 Math Solutions Publications.

Venn Diagram Template

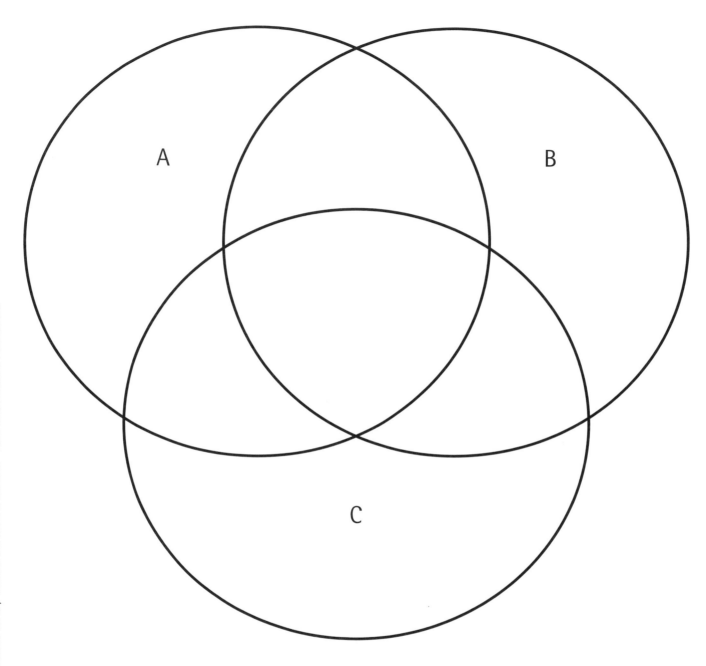

Toy Prices Record Sheet

As reported in *The All-New Book of Lists for Kids*, by Sandra and Harry Choron (New York: Houghton Mifflin, 2002, 133–34) here are the prices of toys in 1897:

Steel blade ice skates	= $ 0.62
Spalding Official Boys' League Baseball	= $ 0.72
Spalding boys' catcher's mitt	= $ 0.20
Solid steel toy wagons	= $ 0.75
Rocking horses	= $ 0.75
Deck of Tally-Ho playing cards	= $ 0.13
Brass band harmonica	= $ 0.22
Girls' 20-inch, two-wheel bicycle	= $29.00
Girls' toy brooms	= $ 0.09
Steel toy safe (piggy bank)	= $ 0.25

Fill in the table below. The projected cost is what the item would cost today, based on the inflation since 1897. The actual cost is the price you have found for that item now. To find the percent increase or decrease, use the projected cost as the original price.

Item	Projected Cost Today	Actual Cost Today	Percent Increase/Decrease
1.			
2.			
3.			

After analyzing your data, explain whether you think that toys are more affordable today or were more affordable in 1897. Defend your answer using the results in your table.

Inch Grid Paper

Cereal Box Evaluation

Name of Cereal: _____

1. Rationale for the design
   1   2   3   4   5

   Comments:

2. Accuracy in measuring
   1   2   3   4   5

   Comments:

3. Neatness of finished product
   1   2   3   4   5

   Comments:

4. Overall attractiveness of the finished product
   1   2   3   4   5

   Comments:

5. Clarity of explanation
   1   2   3   4   5

   Comments:

From *Math and Nonfiction, Grades 6–8* by Jennifer M. Bay-Williams and Sherri L. Martinie. © 2009 Math Solutions Publications.

If the World Were a Village Topic Cards

Topic: Languages	Topic: Food (Quantity)
Data: 22 Chinese; 9 English; 8 Hindi; 7 Spanish; 4 Arabic; 4 Bengali; 3 Portuguese; 3 Russian	Data: 50 no reliable source of food/water; 20 undernourished; 30 always have enough food/water
Topic: Ages	**Topic: Air and Water**
Data: 10 are under 5; 10 are 5–9; 19 are 10–19; 16 are 20–29; 15 are 30–39; 11 are 30–39; 9 are 50–59; 6 are 60–69; 3 are 70–79; 1 is over 79	Data: 75 have access to safe water; 60 have adequate sanitation; 68 breathe clean air
Topic: Religions	**Topic: Electricity**
Data: 32 Christians; 19 Muslims; 13 Hindus; 12 folk religions; 6 Buddists; 2 global religions; 1 Jew; 15 nonreligious	Data: There are 42 radios; 24 televisions; 30 telephones ($\frac{1}{2}$ cellphones); 10 computers
Topic: Food (Meat)	**Topic: History**
Data: 31 sheep and goats; 23 cows, bulls, oxen; 15 pigs; 3 camels; 2 horses; 189 chickens	Data: 500 BC, 2 people; 1 AD, 3 people; 1000 AD, 5 people; 1500 AD, 8 people; 1650 AD, 10 people; 1800 AD, 17 people; 1900 AD, 32 people; 2002 AD, 100 people

From *Math and Nonfiction, Grades 6–8* by Jennifer M. Bay-Williams and Sherri L. Martinie. © 2009 Math Solutions Publications.

Approximating Pi Record Sheet

1. Find the relationship between the circumference and the diameter of these circles using the two strategies described in the book *The Joy of π*, by David Blatner (New York: Walker, 1997).

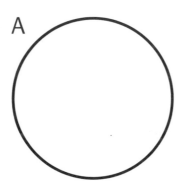

A

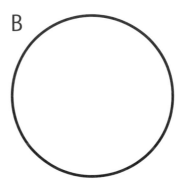

B

2. Find the relationship between the circumference and the diameter of these circles using one of the strategies from above. Record your data in a table.

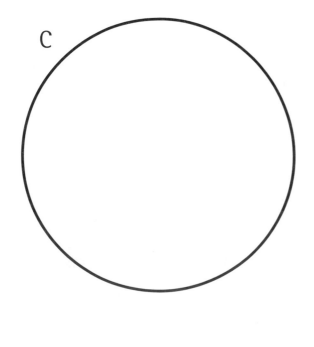

C

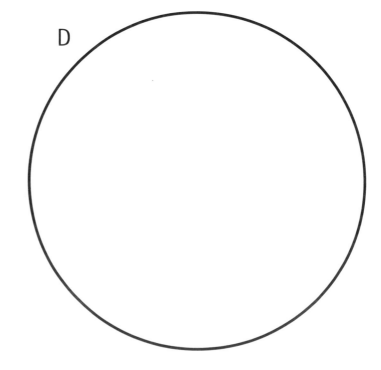

D

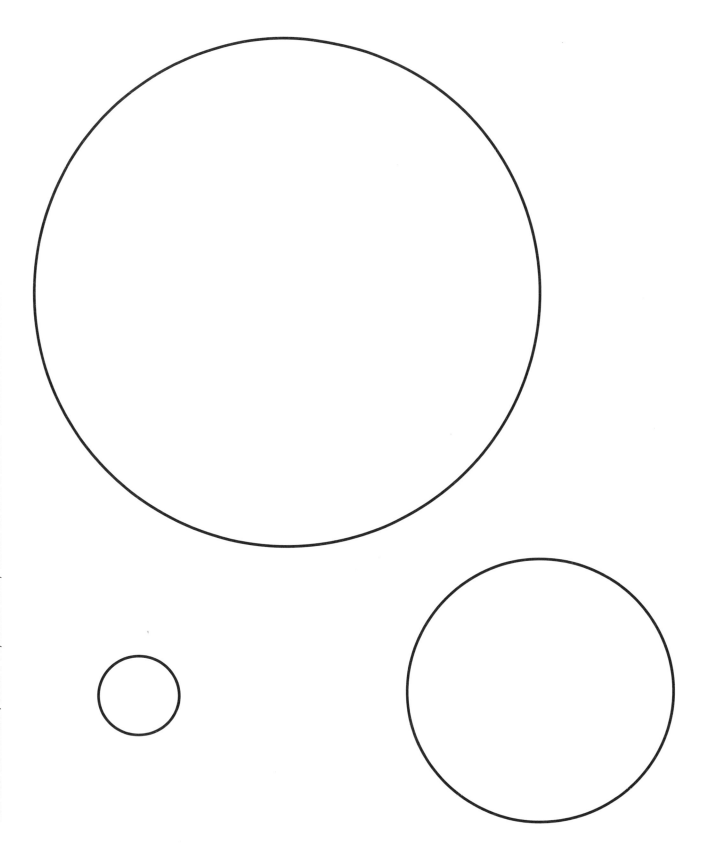

Leonardo's Horse Record Sheet

When a model was made for Leonardo's horse, it was $\frac{1}{8}$ the size of the intended statue.

1. If a three-dimensional cubic model is created with a length of 2 inches, multiplying by 8 gives the actual cube length of 16 inches. Predict the factor that each of the following will increase by:

   Surface Area: _____

   Volume: _____

   Weight: _____

2. Build each of the following model cubes. Record its measurements below:

Length of Side	Base Area	Surface Area	Volume
2			
3			
4			
5			

3. Use grid paper or a graphing calculator to graph the following relationships:

   (x_1, y_1) = (length of side, area of base)

   (x_2, y_2) = (length of side, surface area)

   (x_3, y_3) = (length of side, volume)

From *Math and Nonfiction, Grades 6–8* by Jennifer M. Bay-Williams and Sherri L. Martinie. © 2009 Math Solutions Publications.

4. Which of these relationships are linear? Quadratic? Cubic? Other? Explain this in terms of the physical model growing.

_____

_____

_____

_____

5. Use a separate sheet of paper, or the space below, to describe *to future sculptors* what they need to know about the relationship between the measurements of a model and the final statue when the length of the model is a fraction of the length of the final statue.

The Librarian Who Measured the Earth
Record Sheet

Measurements of Our Circle

Radius:

Diameter:

Circumference:

Angle of sector removed:

Arc length of sector removed:

A. Measure four different sectors and determine the circumference of the circles they came from.

Circle Name	Arc Length (nearest mm)	Angle of Sector (nearest degree)	Circumference of the Circle	Percent Error: Circumference

B. Once you have been given the original measurements, compute the percent error for each circumference.

C. Explain your process for approximating the circumference of a circle.

From *Math and Nonfiction, Grades 6–8* by Jennifer M. Bay-Williams and Sherri L. Martinie. © 2009 Math Solutions Publications.

Made You Look Record Sheet

Magazine Title: _____

Date and Year: _____

Part 1

1. Make a prediction: The percent of advertising in this magazine is _____.

2. Calculate the actual amount of advertising. If necessary, round off to the nearest fourth of a page. The fractional amount of advertising is _____. The percent of advertising is _____.

Part 2

1. Review the advertisements in your magazine. For each ad, decide what type of advertising it uses, for example, "I will be popular if I buy . . ."

2. List that type in the table and record a tally. If you already have that type listed, just record a tally.

3. Complete the chart.

Type of Advertisement	Frequency of Type of Advertisement (Use tally marks.)	Fractional Amount of Advertising	Percent of Advertising

Part 3

Summarize the advertising you found in the magazine. Explain what approaches advertisers most frequently use for young people.

_____

_____

_____

_____

_____

_____

_____

_____

_____

_____

_____

_____

_____

_____

_____

_____

Princess Dido's City Record Sheet

Use the table to record your measurements and areas.

Sketch of Shape	Measurements (for example, length, width, height)	Formula or Strategy for Finding the Area	Area

Imagine the string is 60 yards of fencing that your parents have purchased for making a pen for your pet in your backyard. Explain to your parents the shape(s) you must recommend and the shape(s) that should be avoided if you want a pen that provides a lot of space for your pet.

_____

_____

_____

_____

_____

_____

_____

_____

_____

Guidelines for Favorite Number Report

Part A

Decide upon a favorite number. Keep in mind that you will be writing a feature article about how special this number is. You will need to complete the following steps.

1. Identify the following characteristics of your number:

   factors   prime factorization
   prime or composite   multiples
                            squares

2. Describe at least *three other facts* about your number.

3. Explain why you selected the number.

Part B

Research and explore features of your number. Websites to check out include

http://richardphillips.org.uk/number
http://athensohio.net/reference/number

When you find information from a website, site that source by copying the URL and pasting it into your article at the end.

Part C

Write your feature article. Be creative! Remember:

- the audience (readers of a newspaper, not students in this class)

- the purpose (why your number is interesting, special, unique)

- style (include an introduction, a body, and a conclusion)

- visual support (What visuals should you add to your article to show off your number?)

From *Math and Nonfiction, Grades 6–8* by Jennifer M. Bay-Williams and Sherri L. Martinie. © 2009 Math Solutions Publications.

What Happened to the Mammoths? Record Sheet

Temperature (Celsius)	26°	28°	30°	32°	34°	36°
Number of Eggs	50	100	100	100	100	50
Number of Females Born	10	96	97	85	0	0
Number of Males Born	0	0	0	13	94	7
Number of Eggs That Died	40	4	3	2	6	43

1. What patterns do you notice in the table?

2. Using the chart above, find the ratio of males to females for each temperature reading.

Temperature	Ratio of Males Born to Females Born
26°	
28°	
30°	
32°	
34°	
36°	
Total	

3. Explain the process for changing a part-to-part ratio to a part-to-whole ratio.

_____

_____

_____

_____

_____

_____

References

Arnold, Shannon Jackson. 2004. *Everybody Loves Ice Cream: The Whole Scoop on America's Favorite Treat.* Cincinnati: Emmis Books.

Ball, Johnny. 2005. *Go Figure! A Totally Cool Book About Numbers.* New York: DK.

Blatner, David. 1997. *The Joy of π.* New York: Walker.

Buckley, James Jr., and Robert Stremme. 2006. *Scholastic Book of Lists: Fun Facts, Weird Trivia, and Amazing Lists on Nearly Everything You Need to Know!* Santa Barbara, CA: Scholastic.

Burleigh, Robert. 2002. *Chocolate: Riches from the Rainforest.* New York: Harry N. Abrams.

Choron, Sandra, and Harry Choron. 2002. *The All-New Book of Lists for Kids.* New York: Houghton Mifflin.

Coerr, Eleanor, 1977. *Sadako and the Thousand Paper Cranes.* New York: G. P. Putnam's Sons.

———. *Sadako.* Illus. Ed Young. New York: Putnam & Grosset.

de Paola, Tomie. 1978. *The Popcorn Book.* New York: Holiday House.

Dewdney, A. K. 1993. *200% of Nothing: An Eye-Opening Tour Through the Twists and Turns of Math Abuse and Innumeracy.* New York: John Wiley and Sons.

Dunham, William. 1994. *The Mathematical Universe: An Alphabetical Journey Through the Great Proofs, Problems, and Personalities.* New York: John Wiley and Sons.

Editors of *Yes Mag.* 2004. *Fantastic Feats and Failures.* Toronto: Kids Can.

Fritz, Jean. 2001. *Leonardo's Horse.* Illus. Hudson Talbott. New York: G. P. Putnam's Sons.

Gardner, David, and Tom Gardner. 2002. *The Motley Fool Investment Guide for Teens: Eight Steps to Having More Money Than Your Parents Ever Dreamed Of.* New York: Simon and Schuster.

Graydon, Shari. 2003. *Made You Look: How Advertising Works and Why You Should Know.* Illus. Warren Clark. New York: Annick.

Hoban, Tana. 2000. *Cubes, Cones, Cylinders, and Spheres.* New York: Greenwillow.

Hoffman, David. 2005. *The Breakfast Cereal Gourmet.* Kansas City, MO: Andrews McMeel.

Ishii, Takayuki. 1997. *One Thousand Paper Cranes: The Story of Sadako and the Children's Peace Statue.* New York: Random House Children's Books.

Landau, Elaine. 2006. *The History of Everyday Life.* Minneapolis: Twenty-First Century Books.

Lasky, Kathryn. 1994. *The Librarian Who Measured the Earth.* Illus. Kevin Hawkes. New York: Little, Brown.

Lewis, Leslie D. 2007. "Irrational Numbers Can 'In-Spiral' You." *Mathematics Teaching in the Middle School* 12 (8), 442–446.

Murphy, Patricia J. 2007. *Telling Time.* New York: DK.

Myers, Jack. 2000. *What Happened to the Mammoths? And Other Explorations of Science in Action.* Illus. John Rice. Honesdale, PA: Boyds Mills.

Pappas, Theoni. 1997. *Mathematical Scandals.* San Carlos, CA: Wide World/Tetra.

Phillips, Richard. 2004. *Numbers: Facts, Figures and Fiction.* Evesham, England: Badsey.

Quinn, Robert J. 2001. "Using Attribute Blocks to Develop a Conceptual Understanding of Probability." *Mathematics Teaching in the Middle School* 6 (5): 290–94.

Schwager, Tina, and Michele Schuerger. 1999. *Gutsy Girls: Young Women Who Dare.* Minneapolis, MN: Free Spirit.

Schwartz, David M. 1989. *If You Made a Million.* Illus. Steven Kellogg. New York: Mulberry.

———. 1998. *G Is for Googol: A Math Alphabet Book.* Illus. Marissa Moss. Berkeley, CA: Tricycle.

———. 1999. *If You Hopped Like a Frog.* Illus. James Warhola. New York: Scholastic.

Smith, David J. 2002. *If the World Were a Village: A Book About the World's People.* Illus. Shelagh Armstrong. Tonawanda, NY: Kids Can.

van Sicklen, Margaret. 2005. *The Joy of Origami*. New York: Workman.

Wishinsky, Frieda. 1999. *The Man Who Made Parks: The Story of Parkbuilder Frederick Law Olmsted*. Illus. Song Nan Zhang. Toronto: Tundra Books.

Weatherford, Carole Boston. 2005. *A Negro League Scrapbook*. Honesdale, PA: Boyds Mills.

Index